Running to the Mountain

Running to the Mountain

TO THE

Mountain

A JOURNEY OF
FAITH
AND CHANGE

JON KATZ

VILLARD ❦ NEW YORK

Villard Books and colophon are registered trademarks of Random House, Inc.

LIBRARY OF CONGRESS CATALOGING-IN-PUBLICATION DATA

Katz, Jon.
Running to the mountain: a journey of faith and change / Jon Katz.
    p.   cm.
ISBN 0-679-45678-3 (alk. paper)
1. Katz, Jon—Religion.   2. Novelists, American—20th century—
Biography.   3. Middle-aged men—United States—Biography.
4. Merton, Thomas, 1915–1968—Influence.   5. Journalists—
United States—Biography.   6. Midlife crisis—Religious aspects.
7. Mountain life—United States.   8. Solitude.   I. Title.
PS3561.A7558Z77   1999   813'.54—dc21   98-35229
[B]

This book is for Jeff, Michele,
Milo, Georgia, and Lulu

The madman runs to the East

and his keeper runs to the East;

both are running to the East.

Their purposes differ.

——Z E N   P R O V E R B

THE MORE THINGS CHANGE...

*Struggle in my heart all week. My own moral con-
flict never ceases. Knowing I cannot and must not
simply submit to the standards imposed on me, and
merely conform as "they" would like. This I am
convinced is wrong—but the pressure never ceases.*

—THOMAS MERTON,
TURNING TOWARD THE WORLD

WHEN IT COMES to change, I'm not a detached ob-
server; I'm a partisan.

It can happen: human beings can look inward, face the
realities of their existences, and—sometimes—alter, enrich,
or transform the circumstances under which they live.

They can dream, and—sometimes—they can pursue and
realize their visions.

Few of us can have much influence on the changes in the world beyond our own experiences, the greater physical, economic, or international upheavals. But dealing with the other kind of change, the personal variety, is a nearly universal human drama and preoccupation—and sometimes the stuff of real adventure.

I REMEMBER ALMOST the very moment that the notion of change penetrated my consciousness.

It was a midwinter day in 1959. I was eleven years old, and as happened two or three times a week, I was running for my life through a vast cemetery near North Main Street in Providence, Rhode Island. A pack of fleet-footed and unfriendly kids was hot on my heels. I was gasping, winded, and frightened.

In that less sensitive era, being harassed and thumped by bullies was not considered abuse or even especially dramatic; it was simply the dues paid by any awkward, brooding nerd: a social poll tax, as much a part of life as vegetables or homework.

In self-protection, I'd developed alternate routes home from school: through the cemetery or via a circuitous passage through the backyards and side streets of the East Side. The cemetery provided better protection, with its thousands of tombstones and vaults to hide behind. I knew by heart—still know—many of the French-Canadian names engraved there, depending on the size and complexity of their arrangements for eternity.

My favorite hiding spot was behind the Raychaud family monument, especially the looming marker for the head of the clan, Patrick.

On that bitter cold day, I stuck my head up from behind the granite headstone to see if the way was clear. Too soon. There were shouts, the thumping of sneakers on the frozen ground, and I was overtaken. Soon a gap-toothed redhead was sitting on my chest, thumping me on the side of the head with a schoolbook, calling me a sissy and worse.

The pummeling didn't last long. I was not an exciting or interesting pummelee; I simply went mute and limp. My father had once advised me that when encountering a bully I should attack furiously and let him know that I'd fight; then he'd go pick on somebody else. So, early on, I'd slugged one of these Irish kids, and he'd beaten me silly, thus teaching me a much more valuable lesson.

I had since settled on a more Gandhian response, realizing that the less you seemed to care, the less your tormentors did.

This particular day, the kid sitting on me suddenly got up and turned to listen to one of his pals, who'd come running down the path, panting, red-faced, excited, shouting some news.

"Hey, Buddy Holly is dead," he puffed. "So are Ritchie Valens and the Big Bopper. There was a plane crash somewhere. I heard it in school."

I took great pride in the fact that the Irish kids had made me sniffle but never really cry. But that day I rolled onto my stomach, stuck my face in the snow, and bawled. I was truly wounded, so grief-stricken that the gang, startled, walked away.

Buddy Holly, the young Texas-born singer and composer, a founding hero of rock and roll, was the first person to mean the world to me. His songs went straight to the heart. He was my idol, hope personified, a skinny nice guy with big glasses, the anti-Elvis. Sweet-spirited, stirring, promising not to fade away, Holly heralded something big, some enormous change on the horizon. He was a prophet.

The loss of a powerful presence can crush even the strongest spirit. And I didn't have the strongest spirit. I was overcome that day, and not by a pack of Irish kids.

Even then, I knew something important had happened, not just in that Iowa cornfield but in my own mind. I began to learn about change, to see that loss and eventual renewal were not interruptions of life, they *were* life. Stricken, opened up in a new way, I saw how things on the outside could transfigure me inside, permit me to feel things I hadn't known were there, raise possibilities I hadn't imagined.

In what was probably my first encounter with something akin to spirituality, I saw that I would have to cope with great change, some of it unwanted and unpleasant. I saw that life continued despite it. That the more deeply I felt wounded, the farther inside myself I could see.

It was an awful feeling, yet oddly exhilarating. Even as I grieved for my fallen hero, I felt fiercely alive, and I wanted to feel that alive again. It was a long time before I learned that a plane didn't have to crash for me to experience that sensation. Falling in love did it. Getting married. Having a child. Writing a book. Making a friend.

The world did not come to an end, as I felt it had lying behind the Raychaud family gravestones. Quite the opposite. Much as I loved him, Buddy Holly's death turned out to be a sad note but not the whole song.

Change, from that day, got my attention, changed the way I looked at things. I pored over the news accounts for weeks. The idea that Buddy Holly, just as his career was soaring, could die in some remote snow-covered Iowa field in a blizzard, after the crash of a tiny plane he had decided to board at the very last minute, reordered my world.

If that could happen to Buddy Holly, I didn't dare think about what could happen to me or how little protection or control I had in my own life.

Decades later, when conversations turn to that other generational milestone and people ask where I was when John Kennedy was shot, I can't precisely remember. Kennedy's death simply reinforced a lesson I had already learned.

Holly's loss—and my survival nonetheless—had taught me that the world never stops. That nothing in it is really static or safe, that no loss should be truly shocking. And, of course, that time really is short, sometimes much shorter than you think.

This idea was liberating, not depressing. It told me I could escape from my circumstances.

I've mourned Buddy Holly ever since; I still can't watch a movie about him without dissolving in tears. Yet out of his life and loss, not all at once but over time, change became an enduring reality, a significant factor in my life. It still is.

I can't entirely blame my need for change on Buddy Holly. I'm a restless man and have been, at various points, a troubled one.

Those first stirrings weren't an intellectual position but a survival reflex, an insight provided by the death of a pioneer rocker halfway across the country and by my desire to be someplace—anyplace—other than where I was.

Since then I've had many incarnations. I drove an ice cream truck, then worked as a reporter and editor, briefly became a producer and then a professor. I gave my attention to raising a child and to writing. I've lived in Providence, Boston, Philadelphia, Dallas, Baltimore, Washington, New York, and New Jersey. I've written novels and mysteries, nonfiction books, criticism, essays, and hundreds of columns. I rarely look back, cling to few connections from the past, miss very little of what used to be.

Over time, I have come to believe deeply in the power of change—which is not to say that change is inevitably positive, has always been good for me and those around me, or should be thoughtlessly embraced. A blind belief in change is reckless, a kind of fanaticism. But considered change is sometimes an opportunity.

All that's what running to the mountain in the summer of 1997 was about: change in the service of risk and discovery. Change in search of what the Trappist monk and writer Thomas Merton called the interior life. Change in the pursuit of hope, faith, spiritual meaning.

. . .

FOR ME, BEGINNINGS and ends blend so blurrily I can rarely see the boundaries between one and the other. When my daughter was young, I left my media career behind to become a writer working at home and helping to care for her. This was an enormous change, and a beginning.

But it was also an end. I stopped moving around the country. I stopped taking on and learning new jobs, experiencing new places. I met few new people.

Every day, year after year, I walked my dogs around my block, three or sometimes four times a day. Now and then I varied the route, but over time each variation became so familiar it hardly mattered. The school buses rumbled by each weekday morning at the same time. I shopped at the same markets, ate at the same restaurants, went to the same few movie theaters.

This interruption of the change I'd always pursued was in some ways beneficial. It allowed me to undergo psychoanalysis and confront some of my most serious problems. It permitted me to become a writer. It gave me a chance to focus on trying to be a good father, who truly knew his daughter, and a supportive husband, whose wife could then pursue her own career. Change was hardly absent: my daughter, for example, was evolving constantly, my wife embarking on various adventures. Yet as I eased into a series of routines, I started to feel subsumed, like a twig slowly sinking below the surface of the pond.

My own life was slowing down, perhaps even standing still. I began, as stable, responsible people often do, to feel circumscribed by social obligation and convention. I went to class picnics and parent-teacher conferences. The parents of my daughter's friends invited us for dinner; we invited them. People I ran into on the street mostly seemed to want to talk about their kids. How was mine doing? And theirs? How did we like our schools? The sixth-grade math teacher? We absolutely *had* to get together! More and more, we had drifted into the baby boomer habit of defining ourselves by our children, rather than by the things we ourselves were doing. Sometimes, I thought, I could almost see the people around me disappear into their children's lives, their expectations and identities swallowed almost whole by the experience of having children.

On Fridays my wife and I went out to dinner and a movie. Sundays we had dinner with friends. Saturdays, we split up and raced around all day doing chores. The details of life were mundane yet so complicated that it was hard to step back and consider other possibilities. Always there was the feeling of being pulled along with little control or direction. Even with just one child, there was so much distraction, work, and responsibility. Besides, it felt comfortable. Sometimes it even felt safe.

My instincts for change had softened, matured, as is supposed to happen when you have a family and, in that awfully final phrase, "settle down." I had settled down. Any more settling and I would vanish into the mud like some fat old catfish.

Still, I never stopped missing change. I pined and longed for it like some mooning lover aching after an abruptly ended affair. I feared that my writing was reflecting this new stasis, that it was stale, undernourished by new experience. That I was understimulated, unprovoked by escapades or challenges or even much thought. I fantasized about writing different things, moving to new places, finding a farm in Vermont or a shack in Key West.

But more and more, I told myself, I had to acknowledge the reality of my life, which was that I was getting older, gaining responsibilities, piling up obligations. And nobody else in my family was dreaming about Vermont or Key West.

In fact, most of the people around me seemed to be struggling hard *not* to change—to keep marriages intact, to hold on to their jobs, to hoard money for the inevitable rainy day.

The few times I expressed disenchantment, even to close friends, I heard that dreadful term "midlife crisis." People laughed, rolled their eyes, commiserated, patronized. Wouldn't it be nice to change? But middle-class life was complicated, health care was expensive, and college tuition bills were just around the corner.

It was as if any impulse to step outside one's cautious, predictable life was a sign of trouble. I marveled again at how swiftly and surely much of our culture finds ways to slap down people, young and old, who want to change. Change is impulsive, foolish, dangerous.

If it were true that I needed to change, or even wanted to, all the encouragement I needed would have to come from me. It had to be the interior kind, that spiritual thing.

And this, perhaps, was the critical part. I am not a religious person. Judaism, the faith of my parents, never spoke to me. Too much ritual, an angry and dogmatic God. I began attending Quaker meetings when I was a kid and joined a meeting as an adult. But sooner or later, people like me run into the same wall when it comes to organized religion: those around us all claim to believe in God, and we don't.

Yet I never stopped hoping for some spiritual life, sensing that it lurked inside, waiting for the right opportunity to emerge, even if I didn't know what form it might take. It was the key to whatever direction I might seek for my life.

Spirituality is so shrouded in religious association, dogma and symbolism, ritual and edifice, that nonbelievers can't help feeling left out. Most Americans—more than 90 percent—say they believe in God, yet I wonder. I suspect many, like me, would love to but can't.

For us, spirituality is inward, caught up in change and search.

IN RECENT YEARS I could feel the old restlessness surging, struggling to find some voice or vehicle, especially as my daughter took a part-time job, learned to drive, started sending for college catalogues. I wanted my life to be defined by *me*, once again.

Here was a new chance, as I lurched toward fifty, decades away from the cemetery in Providence, to confront change as a great adventure at a critical point in life. Enthralled with the idea of embracing change again, I wanted to find out if it still had things to teach me, if it deserved the high regard and many expectations I held for it.

If this stubborn preoccupation with change was just a sad echo of an adolescent's pain and loss, that was something I wanted to know just as badly.

Circumstances, some brutal, helped to jump-start the process. But I remembered that change is also sometimes a choice. And I chose it.

I bought a tiny cabin at the very tip of a mountain in a remote corner of upstate New York and went there by myself.

I wanted to undertake what William James wrote was the highest calling of any artist: to find that immortal beauty whose presence constituted my innermost soul, if, in fact, I had a soul at all. If not, I needed to know, so I could go about my business again, uncomplainingly accept my fate, and walk my dogs in peace on those familiar streets, nodding to the neighbors and cracking the same jokes about the weather with our mailman.

For me, faith isn't necessarily about religion. It's about dreams—daring to have them and to risk pursuing them. Change is the way we progress from having dreams to achieving them.

The run to the mountain was, to my mind, a drama of faith and change, a compelling necessity, part of a lifelong struggle for peace, balance, and purpose. Change promised all those things but guaranteed none.

I didn't quite have the courage to go entirely alone, not so far or to so unfamiliar a place.

Thomas Merton had written much about interior lives, self-discovery, and the passages of life he called journeys of the soul. Like Buddy Holly, Merton had become an inspiration.

In the summer of 1997, therefore, I took one of those journeys. I ran to a mountain and spent a good chunk of the next six months there, most of that time alone. I went for a lot of different reasons, but mostly, I think, to try to be a better human. I went with a dead monk and two yellow Labradors as my only companions.

Thanks to Paula Span,

Emma Span, Eve Katz,

Ann Godoff, Flip Brophy,

Jane, Leon, and David Deleeuw,

Julius and Stanley.

Thanks to Thomas Merton,

a.k.a. Father Louis,

whose faith and sacrifice

I have only begun to appreciate.

Running
to the
Mountain

ORPHAN IN THE
PROMISED LAND

*We are invited to forget ourselves on purpose,
cast our awful solemnity to the winds,
and join in the general dance.*

—THOMAS MERTON, NEW SEEDS OF CONTEMPLATION

THE HOUSE SITS like an orphan in the promised land, abandoned and forlorn, right at the peak of a mountain that looks from New York State, across a rural valley carpeted with farms, into the green hills of Vermont.

It is sly, revealing itself slowly, like a stripper in a cheap bar. It lies well off a country road, down a dirt drive. Each step of the way, you feel swallowed up a bit more by the forest; the world gets left further behind.

The first thing I saw was an odd tide of almost eerie debris—decaying benches, rotting wagon wheels, a sign that said THE LAST RESORT hanging askew on a pole. The lawn was baked and dusty, half dead, the gardens overgrown and untended.

Here and there posts that had once supported birdhouses stuck up from the ground. I counted half a dozen stacks of firewood, enough for three or four winters, scattered around.

A tall plastic swimming pool full of scum and slime sat by the side door, and something—a frog, maybe a snake—slid out of it as I came near. My two Labradors and I jumped.

"Jesus, welcome to Dogpatch," I said to my friend Jeff, who lived in a nearby town. Jeff had scouted the house and had strongly urged me to drive north and take a look.

"Wait," he said.

Disappointed, I wondered what he had been thinking, urging me to rush upstate and look at this decrepit, charmless place, a tiny cabin built in 1965. A truck driver and his father had constructed it board by board, all 846 square feet of it, and couldn't have been any prouder if it were the Taj Mahal. I was also relieved to be underwhelmed; I couldn't afford a second house, anyway.

Georgette, the real-estate agent, watching me sag, was murmuring about the possibilities, trying to spark my imagination. "I'd take down the dark paneling," she suggested. "Open it up a bit."

But the interior was even more dispiriting, murky and tomblike, with thick shag carpeting in hideous colors and fake-wood ceiling beams made of plastic. The small kitchen was festooned with ceramic tiles and plaques offering sayings like KISSIN' DON'T LAST, COOKIN' DO.

While showing me how dry the basement was, Georgette asked me to pick up a couple of decomposing mice and toss them out into the woods. My dogs looked unnerved.

Then Jeff took me by the arm, led me past the swampy pool to the front of the house, and rotated me eastward. The sight hit me like a hammer blow; I almost reeled. The view was as spectacular and uplifting as the approach from the rear was cheesy and disheartening.

What a tease this house was, betraying no hint of where it really was. The lakes and farmland spread out for miles before us. I could see tiny dairy cows grazing deep in the valley. Mist shrouded the hills opposite, and sunbeams streaked from the sky and lit up the distant mountaintops.

Jeff said nothing, letting the view speak for itself. I sat down on the front step and tried to take it in.

My dogs, I could see, were transformed. The older Lab, Julius, a philosopher and contemplative, plopped down and didn't move, staring hypnotically at a hawk floating above the valley. Julius was born to muse and observe. He has never chased a ball, retrieved a stick, treed a squirrel, entered water deeper than his ankles, run more than a few yards, or menaced any creature.

Stanley is another story. He has a devilish lust for mischief and for retrieving, amassing caches of socks, underwear, and chew bones. He is happy to chase rubber balls till he drops. Less regal but far more energetic, Stanley went right to work and rushed into the woods to collect sticks.

I felt transformed, too. In a few seconds I had gone from not being able to imagine living in this neglected dump to not believing that somebody like me could possibly be lucky enough to own it.

"It's a writer's place," said Jeff. "The view is worth a million bucks. The house, you can always fix up."

That was right, I thought, seizing on the idea, the reassuring real estate truisms. The land, not the house. Buy land, they're not making any more of it. It's an investment, not an expense. What difference did the carpeting make anyway, when you could gaze at *this* outside?

I almost drooled at the prospect of toting my computer up here, clacking away in the shade of the maple in the back-yard. I had the sensation of something important happening to me. It was a familiar feeling.

TEN YEARS EARLIER, as executive producer of the two-hour program *The CBS Morning News,* I had stood in a control room one day before dawn, staring at a wall of high-tech color monitors. The coanchor of the spectacularly unsuccessful show, a former beauty queen and sports commentator named Phyllis George, was smiling back at me surreally from all of them. An assistant dabbed at her makeup and fluffed her hair.

I was powerful, well compensated, lost.

A few minutes later, I was locked in my office, weeping. I had reached a rung in life a lot of people would have coveted, and I would rather have thrown myself off a bridge than stay there for another month.

So, tentatively, with equal parts determination and terror, I set out on what Thomas Merton liked to call a journey of the soul.

Merton, a Trappist monk whose work I had begun reading when I was in the ninth grade and in sore need of solace, as did millions of others all over the world, was my guide on this trip. I'd read almost everything he'd written. He was a Catholic, I was raised a Jew; he had absolute faith, I never did. Still, for reasons I may never completely understand, he spoke to me, personally and powerfully. As a boy, I'd written him a letter that he never answered; if he had, I might have wound up in the monastery with him. Merton died thirty years ago. I never met him, but if a stranger's voice can enter one's soul, his permeated mine.

"It is absolutely impossible," he wrote all those years ago, "for a man to live without some kind of faith."

It is equally impossible to change your life without some.

A prolific author, journal keeper, letter writer, and poet, Merton lived in the abbey of Gethsemani in the Kentucky woods. He was approaching fifty when he retreated to a hermitage; perhaps it's not coincidental that as I approached fifty, I ran to a mountain, too.

Merton was obsessed with a central issue for our time— figuring out how to live, trying to forge a life of purpose and meaning. I've grown to share his obsession, his belief that life demands a lot of tinkering, requires people to give birth to themselves not just once but over and over.

Central to much of Merton's writing is the idea of these journeys, powerful images of seeking and traveling. The journey of the soul—his term—is to me one of his most important notions. It has enormous moral force and potent appeal to us wretched pilgrims as we struggle to find direction, to figure out what to believe, to incorporate some measure of spirituality and peace into our frantic lives.

Our approaches could hardly have been more different, of course. If he accepted dogma, I find much of it the antithesis of reason. He struggled to remain behind monastery walls, while for me, everything depends on getting over the walls.

Nevertheless, in the years since I stared into those monitors, my own journey had proceeded, my life changing more radically than I had imagined.

I underwent years of psychoanalysis, became a writer, and swore never to work for a large institution again. Shedding ambitions, friends, and colleagues of fifteen years, I left the world of offices, annual evaluations, meetings, suits, and expense accounts behind for good.

The world I entered—the life of a suburban parent and solitary author—could not have been more different. I crossed a vast cultural and social divide in months, from barking orders in a high-tech control room to holing up in the attic of my house trying to write and sell a novel, keeping one eye on the clock so I never missed a car pool.

Had I a realistic idea of what a writer's life would really be like, I would have thought a lot longer and harder.

But the point was, I began one year a big-deal producer and ended it at home, fielding calls about play dates from the other moms, learning the ways of supermarkets, and sitting in front of a primitive Apple computer at the dawn of the Digital Age, clacking out the story of a network taken over by a heartless conglomerate.

So began the wildest ride of my life.

A decade, seven books, and countless articles later, I was driving up the New York State Thruway, my heart pounding like some eager traveler about to hit the road again.

Change, I remembered all too well, is risky and frightening as well as exciting and rewarding. Much as you flail around seeking help, when it's all said and done, there is only one genuine source of inspiration, courage, and determination—that's you.

But as I turned fifty in the summer of 1997, even before I stood on that mountain, I already suspected that I needed to take another trip, even if I didn't really know why.

In fact, this spiritual adventure, running to the mountain, proved even more frightening than the first. A decade of shocks, disappointments, successes, and defeats had accumulated since the last trip. If I had a heightened sense that one could successfully change one's life, being a writer had taught me time and again that rejection and failure were even greater possibilities. The first time, I'd leaped more or less blindly into the void. This time, I had a sense of what awaited me.

Only recently has it occurred to me that recounting this ongoing trek might be worthwhile. Because so many people have embarked on journeys of their own—of all sorts, from parenthood or divorce to changing a career and facing the end of life—it may be worth telling.

I HAD TO have this house; once I saw the view, I knew that right away and I never wavered. But I had plenty of dread and guilt, even panic, about proceeding. It was far from clear that this was the right thing to do. My wife would be upset and unhappy. I had bills to pay. It was the worst possible time for my daughter, a high school student heading for an undoubtedly expensive college.

If there is a Code of Responsibility for somebody like me,

a middle-class man living a middle-class life in a middle-class New Jersey town, acquiring another house at this point would violate most of its provisions.

The conventional wisdoms went ricocheting around my mind: Family comes first. Responsible people pay outstanding debts before taking on new obligations. We had to fix up the wreck of a house we already owned before we took on a new wreck. We should think about saving for retirement. In a writer's wobbly financial life, the only predictable thing is that nothing is predictable.

When a person with a family takes a gamble like this, he is playing with more than his own fate, of course. If he guesses wrong, the people he loves most go down with him.

So buying this house was an ass-backward move, premature, unjustifiable. I could already hear my friends. *What is he thinking? Is this a midlife crisis? Poor Paula.*

Poor Paula. An inherently steady and responsible woman, she had married an unstable maniac, but she hadn't figured that out until it was too late. That she had not grabbed a toothbrush and run for her life a hundred times is a source of continuing astonishment.

We'd moved nine times in the first ten years of our marriage. Our lives lurched from one work crisis—all mine—to another. Now Paula and I not only had no money to spare, we were in debt—again. We were just beginning to bounce back from a nightmarish family trauma—our daughter had undergone major surgery the year before—that was both draining and costly. The last thing we needed was another mortgage.

The truth is, I'm still sorting out why I felt compelled to retreat to the mountain. I'm sure it had something to do with my birthday looming just a few weeks away. If I didn't feel old, exactly, I was increasingly conscious of age. I wouldn't have many more chances to further recast my life.

I'm not nearly as afraid of dying as I am of the hinges inside my mind and soul rusting closed. I am desperate to keep them open, because I think that if they close, that's one's first death, the loss of hope, curiosity, and possibility, the spiritual death. After that, it seems to me, the second one is just a formality. I wanted to oil the hinges, force the doors to stay open.

As a writer I was reasonably successful but almost too busy. To make enough money to live, I was writing constantly— books, articles, columns on a Web site, some good stuff and some not so. I wanted, needed more space to think and write. I needed to do fewer things better in the time I had remaining.

I wanted to try harder to figure out how a rational human being sets out on his or her own, to find a faith and an ethical code. I wanted some real peace.

I wanted to change the script I saw being written for me. I believed that was possible because I'd done it before.

I didn't want to spend the rest of my days cranking out articles and books in northern New Jersey, clacking away at the keyboard, whittling away at my bills, until I keeled over.

Yet, I could picture that happening. Sometimes I had dreams about it. I saw myself taking my affable dogs for their final walk of the night on my quiet suburban street, where we walked four or five times every day and knew each tree, shrub, and manhole cover. Overweight and out of shape, I would feel tightness in my chest. I would sweat, totter, fall to the ground, wishing I'd brought my cell phone. The dogs would pace anxiously, confused at this unusual behavior as I lay on the sidewalk, gasping for breath. Stanley would probably bring me a stick. But Julius, who lies close by my side every second when I'm sick, would know exactly what was happening. He'd sit down next to me, whining and licking my face.

Sometimes, in this vision, Paula has fallen asleep on the couch watching the late news as I lie there wishing I had some way to scribble a final message. Sometimes I die right on the sidewalk, worrying that I haven't said good-bye to my family, hoping the dogs get home somehow.

In alternate visions, Paula wakes up, notices my absence, and comes out looking for me. Sometimes I hear the sympathetic murmurs of concerned neighbors as the ambulance pulls away.

I don't want to die in New Jersey.

It's become my mantra, evolving from a fantasy to a kind of recurring panic. It isn't that New Jersey is a bad place, or that I much care where I actually draw my last breath. But the symbolism is bell-ringing: this isn't how I want things to end, any more than producing a network TV show had been a decade earlier. Leaving TV to be a parent, a writer working at home, a man who knew how to shop and cook, was the right choice for me when I made it. But it was a chapter, not the whole story; a means, not an end. I'd done it, and again I wanted something more.

So in 1997, against all reason, I bought the house and ran to the mountain. The people who knew me best were the most amazed. I've lived in big cities most of my life—New York, Washington, Boston, Philadelphia, Baltimore—until my daughter was born, when we moved to a suburb outside New York.

I've had little to do with the country or nature. My favorite night out is a trip to a bookstore, the pizza place, and the Sony megaplex twenty minutes from my house. I have rarely lived in isolation, am unable to fix or maintain much of anything. There are men who know how things work and men who never learned; I am one of the latter.

But I'm proud of the fact that I have been taking a journey of the soul; I've become part of a secret society of travelers, spiritual adventurers. En route, I've struggled mightily to figure out how to be spiritual without having to be religious, how to find peace without bending my knee before an altar.

And on this particular part of the trip, I have lots of company.

People like me are drawn again and again to sacred books, holy men, and revealed words. Then we almost inevitably become confused, disillusioned, frustrated. We pull back. We are too skeptical to submit to absolute faith, much as we might want to.

But we can't, as Merton suggests, live without faith altogether. So we bounce back and forth from one state to the other, spiritual refugees, adrift in a void. We can't let go because we badly want a spiritual framework for our lives; we can't, don't even dare, believe we might find truths on our own; we look everywhere else for answers. We want change and fear it.

We are a lonely generation in that way. We don't have wise men and women to guide us, traditions to follow. The lives, truths, and experiences of our parents often don't help us any more than those of priests and rabbis. The world has changed too quickly; we know it and it frightens us. We are afraid to let the old trappings go, but we know we're heading out without a map.

Standing on that mountain that day, I had what my old friend Merton might call a revelation. Since in many ways my own journey began with him, why not take a trip with him, a spiritual adventure—up here? Why not test and, I hoped, affirm my faith in me? Why not run to the mountain with a PowerBook and tackle the questions that have been buzzing in my brain for years, questions so many others have been gnawing at: Do you have to be a monk to be a holy man? Can you find spirituality outside of a church, temple, or mosque? Is it possible to build a rational, moral framework for your life amidst the choices, complexities, pressures, expenses of modern existence? How healthy is change? How much is too much?

So I accepted the invitation to Merton's General Dance. I forgot myself on purpose. I took a chance, cast my awful solemnity to the winds, and broke for the mountain.

BOOMER SHOCK

Run to the mountain;
Shed those scales on your eyes
That hinder you from seeing God

—DANTE, "PURGATORIO," *THE DIVINE COMEDY*

WHO KNOWS WHERE journeys really begin?

These trips, these journeys of the soul and adventures in change, often begin unhappily, born of pain, disappointment, or shock. When we're suffering, we're often more receptive and amenable to change; we feel things more acutely. It's easier to shed the scales from our eyes. When things are going well, it's natural that we close up.

I'm a spiritual bottom-feeder: When trouble comes, I start sniffing right away for the possibilities. Grief opens you up, gets you thinking, wishing for a God to turn to.

My trek to the mountain might have started decades ago, when my sister broke down abruptly and we, the closest of siblings, became strangers, and my family fell apart.

But when I search my memory for a moment, an event, that began the process, I usually picture the cheerful pastel waiting room of the Hospital for Special Surgery in New York City.

Paula and I, two obsessively verbal people, were beyond words. She, who doesn't read much fiction, was immersed in

Jane Austen. I, who don't have much taste for classical music, was listening to Mozart on a CD player with headphones.

We were profoundly alone together, looking perhaps a bit wistfully at an extended Eastern European clan across the room whose ranks swelled all day as, down the hall, a matriarch or patriarch went under the knife.

This was, for us, the longest day. We were waiting while our daughter, Emma, underwent surgery for severe scoliosis, a deformation of the spine.

Learning that Emma needed to have her spine fused with bone grafts and titanium rods had been bad enough. But the context of our times gave it a particularly shocking quality. Paula and I are boomer parents, that special breed that takes all the idealism, education, anxiety, and insanity of the sixties and focuses it on our children like a powerful beam. Emma was an only child with two parents on perpetual Defcon Five Alert.

The central conceit of boomers is that they can control the world they live in, by one means or another. They not only believe it, they insist upon it. They think they can and should create perfect children who lead lives free of failure, risk, and pain. All the harder the fall when it comes.

Like so many boomer and other kids, Emma is much loved, highly tended-to. She must have visited pediatricians a hundred times, for one ailment or another, in her fourteen years. Whenever she needed immunizations. Whenever she had a fever. Whenever she had a cold that lasted more than three days. Every spring for her camp physical.

This partly explains why we may never completely recover from learning that despite all that vigilance, nobody involved in the booming business of monitoring Emma had recognized that her spine was twisting, and a hump forming on her back.

To discover awful things going on unseen in the very center of your child's body is a savage reminder of our limitations, the boundaries of our ability to protect the people we love.

So there we were, in July of 1996—just a few weeks after her camp physical, when the curvature had finally been paid attention to, then x-rayed and measured—saying good-bye to our daughter outside the doors of the surgical suite.

There is nothing in parental experience that tells you what to say as your kid is wheeled off for a brutal, lengthy operation. The doctors are confident to the point of being blasé. You're afraid she'll be disabled for life. I had rehearsed various presurgical witticisms for days, not wanting to be so heavy-handed that I frightened her or so light that I trivialized what she faced.

I wanted to tell her how much she meant to me without sounding grave or melodramatic. I wanted to be of some use. But some things are just not possible.

We tried for casual. One of the two pediatric anesthesiologists injected some sort of tranquilizer into her IV line and Em went down the hall smiling. "This is how your mother spent the sixties," I joked, and she smiled. I swear I felt my heart crack.

The hospital's waiting room is bright and airy, with a zillion-dollar view of tugboats and barges gliding along the

East River. There's tasteful art on the walls, coffee and tea on a countertop.

To help distract the people waiting, the TV sets scattered here and there stay on all day long. And on this already surreal afternoon, every one of them showed flaming bits of wreckage floating in black water, the same images repeated every few minutes on every screen, hour after hour. It was the morning after TWA Flight 800 had exploded over Long Island Sound.

Paula and I had crossed over to the other side, I remember thinking, staring at the burning debris for the hundredth time. We have left the ranks of the safe and prosperous. I had the strongest sensation that we would never completely return.

We were zombie people, restless and disconnected, saying little, standing up, sitting down, going to the bathroom, making a call, squeezing each other's shoulders in silent resignation.

Why are we always surprised that events like this change us for good, even though it is both obvious and inevitable that they must?

Pieces of me were already rearranging themselves in some cosmic way. I should have expected this. I had already undergone nearly a decade of psychoanalysis. Somebody like me never walks away from something like that unchanged, if anybody does.

But you never can really have enough self-awareness, I keep learning.

Emma bore the brunt of her surgery, of course, but my already patched-together psyche had taken a massive hit and the fragile scaffolding I'd worked for years to build was tottering. I saw life in a fresh, quite vivid way. I had a new sense of time. I'd gotten a Ph.D. in fate.

But as had happened when my media career collapsed years earlier, I was also opened up again. I was thinking about my life, paying attention to it.

The surgery reminded me of what that earlier trip had taught: that life should never be unthinking but that mine had become routinized and reflexive, perhaps a bit lazy. I saw again that all clichés are true, which is why they are clichés. You don't live forever. You can't control fate. Time is precious.

Dealing with crises like these, each in our own way, some people surround themselves with relatives and friends. We were bombarded with offers, generous and sometimes insistent: we should have company, we should let friends visit, talk to us, walk the dogs, help out.

I was beyond that sort of help. Paula allowed a couple of her best girlfriends to bring meals and then steal away, or run some errands at home. I wanted nobody but Paula around; in fact, I couldn't bear it. All I really remember is clinging to her like a drowning man to a piece of driftwood, numb and in terror.

One of the few exceptions was Jeff Goodell, a writer who lived in a corner of upstate New York whose name I could never remember. We'd met through a computer-conferencing system called the WELL, and we'd been friends for nearly a year before we met face-to-face.

Jeff lived nearly an hour northeast of Albany, in an out-of-the-way, slightly tattered, but beautiful town called—okay, I did remember—Cambridge. It sits between the Adirondacks and Vermont, north of Hoosick Falls and south of Salem. It's on the way to nowhere.

Except for Emma's beloved summer camp in Vermont. Cambridge is more or less on the way there, which is probably the only reason I found my way to it at all.

When I finally visited the place the summer before the surgery, having driven Em to camp, I was taken aback. The discomfort at meeting someone I had only known on-line and on the phone lasted all of a minute and a half. But I was surprised to find Jeff, a lanky, easygoing native Californian, and Michele, a Yale grad and political and corporate speechwriter, in a remote, bleak place I immediately labeled Yokumville.

Main Street was five or six blocks long. The police station was smaller than my garage, the nearest movie fifteen miles away, the most accessible Thai take-out in some other state. Trailer homes were nestled in beautiful valleys; rotting shacks with tar-paper windows sat next to regally restored farmhouses.

The bleating I heard in Jeff's backyard came from the sheep farm next door. The smell of manure wafted in through the open windows of the cavernous old house, built before the Revolutionary War and large enough, it seemed, for the whole town. A livestock auction house was located a mile or so down the road, along with a liquor store that took only cash and a roadhouse where people like me were probably distinctly unwelcome.

What was a hip *Rolling Stone* writer, a respected chronicler of the Net and the Web, a child of Silicon Valley, doing in a place like this? Jeff couldn't really tell me how it had happened. He said it was Michele's idea; she said it was his. Even as they squawked about what a white elephant the house was, I could see how deeply attached they were to the place.

I talked to Jeff constantly during the days before, during, and after Emma's surgery, though I remember little of what we said to each other. He says I sounded ghostly, dazed.

And Jeff didn't try to make me feel better. He just called, listened, made sure that I was okay. On the phone, he suggested that when the surgery was over I come up for a visit, to wind down. It sounded enticing.

The operation was more brutal and exhausting than I had expected but even more successful. The surgery completely corrected Emma's wayward spine. She was immediately two inches taller and on the way to a lengthy but full recovery. The surgeon was brandishing her X rays like a trophy. "We had a great day in there," he announced, beaming at us at the end of that long, grim afternoon. So he did.

And after a couple of weeks, as we walked Emma slowly, painfully, across her hospital room, then down the corridor, then down the street we lived on, and then around the block, as she healed and grew stronger, I thought about Yokumville.

I HAD BEEN there two weeks before the surgery, as it happens. Another stop en route to camp.

Even with the operation looming, Emma had hoped to spend a few weeks in Vermont at this place she'd grown to love more each summer, ever since she was a ten-year-old

sleeping in a cabin called Six Pines. But it was proving difficult, she told us in a subdued phone call. I drove up to discuss it.

We went for a walk by the lake. She wanted to stay, she
said, but giving blood, as she'd done each week in prepara-
tion for the surgery, had physically worn her out. It was hard
to get on with the daily business of having fun at camp when
you were facing spinal surgery. She didn't want to bring down
the other kids. She thought she might be better off at home.
I thought she might, too. Relieved of the burden of toughing
it out, she went to tell her counselors she'd be leaving. They
concurred but wanted her to have time for—another boomer
concept—"closure."

So I'd spent a couple of days driving back and forth
between Vermont and Cambridge while Emma found closure
and packed her trunk. Jeff and I took long walks along the
Battenkill River. We got up early for coffee and muffins at
D'Aiuto's Bakery on Main Street. We went into Manchester
to browse through the Northshire Bookstore. We sat out on
his porch at night and listened to the crickets. We ate in ratty
diners where guys with big bellies smoked cigarettes over the
eggs they were frying on greasy black grills.

His friendship, our talks and walks, made a difference to
me. I was all ripped up inside. Things had moved too quickly
for me to deal with any of them—learning about the scoliosis, driving Em here and there for preoperative tests, waiting
to bring her home. At Jeff's I felt better, calmer. Some of it
was him. But some of it, I could sense, was the place.

Yokumville was getting under my skin, creeping into my
soul. I liked the space, the farms and woods. The wooded

roads we hiked, the wild turkeys popping up out of the fields, the deer bounding through meadows. I liked seeing dogs dozing on Main Street in the middle of the day. I especially loved the mountains, which towered above us and framed everything we saw.

The scales began to drop from my eyes, and I was stunned by the beauty of the place, the intensity and proximity of nature.

During that presurgical trip, when I was filled with admiration and apprehension for my game daughter, a bit of me fell in love with Jeff, with our deepening friendship, and a bit of me fell in love with those lovely mountains and streams.

Afterward, returning with a battered but recovering Emma in August, this was no longer Yokumville but a shelter that had seen me through some of the scariest days of my life. Here I saw how much I had been shaken by the surgery. But I also began to heal.

That summer, during the trips that bracketed Emma's surgery, it occurred to me, in the haziest way, that I wanted a refuge of my own here. For years I'd dreamed about having such a place. Now I began to think this was it.

I didn't say a word about it to anybody, not even Jeff. I still poked fun at Yokumville, at cracker life, at trailer parks. I wanted to live, I told him again and again, in a Jersey condo near a mall, equidistant from a good pizza place and a bookstore. That was the life for me. I'd walk the dogs across the vast parking lot.

It's funny, but I see now that the more the mountains appealed to me, the more I invoked my asphalt fantasy. It was a mantra, I suspect, to ward off what was growing inside.

The place had touched me. There I might find some of the things I'd long wanted but rarely had. I'd run one day to a mountain just as Thomas Merton had run to a hermitage. I'd write and think; days would pass marked by long walks in the woods with my dogs, great and unimaginable levels of creativity, and, for good measure, my close friend down below in the valley. I could leave the pain of my family and the struggles of my life far behind.

What a silly fantasy. I was a city boy. I knew little about nature. I was lethal with a keyboard, but I'd barely held a hammer. I had no money to spare. This was merely the predictable escapism of a middle-aged man emerging from the terror and confusion that followed his daughter's hellish ordeal. It would go away, like so many other fantasies I'd cherished, then abandoned—moving to Cape Cod, living the intellectual's life in Cambridge, Massachusetts.

Money considerations ruled out my mountain fantasy, anyway. The surgery had wasted us financially. I was late with various books and articles. We were squabbling with insurance companies. Paula had put up with plenty of financial ups and downs—more of the latter since I'd turned to writing. I thought she would kill me if I even mentioned the idea of a retreat in a place like Cambridge, New York. And nobody would blame her, not even me.

BUT STILL . . . HERE I was, a year later, "just looking" at a house on a mountain. The asking price was a very reasonable seventy-six thousand dollars. It had been on the market for more than a year. I decided to bring up the idea.

Paula was emphatic. We had other priorities. The house could wait. She wanted me to drop it. She also understood me well enough to know that once I started talking money, I was beginning a process that would almost surely end with our signing another mortgage.

"This doesn't make any sense," she said. "Emma's about to go off to college. We don't need to take this on." She made several different tries at dissuading me. Maybe we should wait. Maybe rent for a year. Maybe look at a different, closer area. We went back and forth.

But we'd never told each other what to do. It was, ultimately, up to me. I just wanted to talk, I told her. I feared we'd always have too many good reasons for waiting—debts, bills, college, home repairs, sickness, then old age.

I plotted my strategy in Jeff and Michele's kitchen. A cardinal rule of negotiating is never to bluff; if you have a firm price in mind, declare it and stick to it. Be prepared to walk away. Working in television, watching the killer execs at CBS slash and burn, had taught me something about the process.

I instinctively felt I had the edge in these negotiations. I made sure that Georgette, the real estate agent, knew my wife wasn't sharing this particular dream. I *was* genuinely put off by the house and all the work it needed. The way to feel better about it was to get it so cheaply that rather than endangering my family, I would be acquiring a beautiful piece of property—an investment—for about the price of a new Mercedes sedan.

I thought I was in the driver's seat. I had leverage.

So I called Georgette. Seventy-six thousand was too high, I said. The house was a wreck, the grounds overgrown, and the interior dark and cluttered. It would need a lot of work. Georgette, who was probably in her sixties, blond and carefully coiffed and unflappable, gave nothing away.

She was, I could tell, sincerely worried about the owner. Lenny was anxious to sell the house, she said, but she didn't say why. I knew he was a Long Island truck driver in his forties and that he loved the house, in part because he'd built it with his father. I knew he loved coming north in the winter, stoking the fireplace and holing up for days. I knew he had a young son. Something must be pressuring him to unload it— a lost job, maybe, or health problems, perhaps a divorce.

"I'd like to offer sixty thousand dollars," I said to Georgette. "What about it?" In my mind, that was it; I wouldn't go more than a few dollars higher.

Georgette was cool as dry ice. "Why don't you stop by the office tomorrow and put down a deposit? Something small. That will be a gesture of good faith." She could then call Lenny and say that I was serious about the negotiations, even if he rejected my offer.

I understood, of course, that we had crossed a bridge. I'd left the realm of browsers.

I didn't have any checks with me, so Jeff wrote me one for fifteen hundred dollars, refundable. Driving to Georgette's office on Main Street, I was anxious and guilty. And excited. Leaving the deposit, filling out a raft of forms, I could see that I wasn't really in the driver's seat. I wanted to buy the house at least as badly, if not more, as Lenny wanted to sell it.

Georgette's eyes twinkled. "So you like the view, eh?" She grinned. "I thought you did."

Back at Jeff's, I called Poor Paula, the euphoria I'd felt in the real-estate agent's office gone. She was not angry but resigned. I felt all the more crummy, like a little boy caught stealing.

"I'm sorry," I told my wife, "to keep ruining your life."

OF MEN AND MICE

Lead ahead, Deerslayer, and open the bushes;
the rest I can do for myself.

—JAMES FENIMORE COOPER, *THE DEERSLAYER*

A COUPLE OF days later, waiting for the next install-
ment of this drama to unfold, Jeff and I stopped at the Burger
Den, the family restaurant at the foot of the mountain, for
take-out sandwiches. Then we drove up for another look at
the house I longed for and feared.

It was a sticky, overcast day, the sun drifting in and out of
the heavy clouds. Jeff sat on one side of the rickety old picnic
table and I on the other.

"It's up to you," he said finally, answering the question it
wasn't necessary to ask aloud. "I think you might do some
great writing up here."

I nodded, munching on my tuna sandwich.

Jeff's amber-eyed black mutt, Lulu, tore off into the
woods in pursuit of some poor, doomed creature. Lulu was a
sweet and loyal creature to people she liked but a killing
machine to all other living things. Soon we heard some
piteous shrieking—a mouse or woodchuck, maybe—off in
the woods. Then silence.

Julius and Stanley looked at each other, puzzled as always
as to why any dog would run that fast in the heat, and settled

down to doze. A bolt of sunlight shot out of the sky over the valley.

When Jeff gets excited about an idea or tries to explain what autumn is like upstate or how the mountains change color in winter, his hands begin to circle like windmills.

"You could bring the PowerBook right out here to the picnic table in the morning, especially in August when the flies are gone," he said. "You can sit up here and look across the valley and work all day."

His hands were going full tilt.

BOYS WHO GROW up estranged from their fathers enter the world with particular disabilities. They have trouble with authority, of course. They may abhor shouting and screaming—that's me—or they may mostly communicate that way. They're often uncomfortable with other men.

In one sense, they are doomed. To break with your father means you will never really have peace, never completely come to terms with who you are. Men who grew up with serious and unresolved problems with their fathers are alone in the world in a particular way.

One of the things that first attracted me to Thomas Merton's writings was his moving descriptions of this loneliness. I saw myself in it. And he knew what he was talking about. His parents had both died when he was very young, and his brother—his only sibling—was killed in World War II.

Because no one teaches them, boys like me don't know how to do a lot of things. I lived with an aunt and uncle for a few months when I was a teenager, to complete the school year after my family moved. My uncle was shocked at all I didn't know: how to tie a necktie, polish dress shoes, pack a suitcase, swing a bat, use tools, tell the difference between a Phillips screwdriver and the other kind. "Didn't anybody teach him anything?" he kept asking my mother.

Men this ignorant are crippled; they feel stupid and incompetent. I am exactly the man my father saw clearly and wanted so much to change: someone ill at ease with his own body, someone who has no idea how the machinery works, who grasps none of the rudiments of outdoor life. The things I *can* do well are not things he would have valued.

For these and other reasons, I was the last person you'd expect to buy a decaying handyman's special on the top of a mountain in a remote place. I was the last person to negotiate the complexities of nature or to take the kind of responsibility for myself that living on my own for extended periods would inevitably bring.

Maybe that was one of the reasons I felt so much panic about this place. Lenny had built the house with his father; it was a literal monument to—and result of—family closeness and paternal love. Hanging on the wall near the kitchen was a Father's Day BEST DAD plaque in honor of Lenny's father. Now I, so long estranged from my own father, unable to patch a screen or wire a phone jack, was contemplating living there.

In many ways, Jeff helped me compensate for these sorrows, blank spots, and shortcomings. Jeff is handy. He knows how to put things together—doors, lamps, furniture—and take them apart. He can spot animals in the woods that I wouldn't notice, and he understands the rhythms of nature.

He knows how tools work and which ones to use. And he is gentle and patient about passing along the things he knows.

So, like a father, he taught me.

He is also a writer, of course, sharing with me the innumerable ups and downs—financial perils, rejected ideas, manuscripts that need more work, the teeth-grinding envy of watching thirty-year-olds get million-dollar publishing contracts.

So, he was a peer.

More than that, we had both lost siblings. Jeff's brother died painfully and young of AIDS. His father had died shortly before that of lung cancer. I had lost a brother and sister, too, though they were alive. Like mine, Jeff's family had been nearly destroyed and was now scattered to the winds.

So, he was a brother.

We watched out for each other, worried about each other, were available to each other, trusted each other in an unquestioning way, like the Hardy boys or buddies in a John Wayne movie.

So, above all, he was a friend.

If traumas tend to open us up, friends help keep us that way, showing and teaching, coaxing us out of our own experiences, giving us the strength to take a chance and helping us heal when we fall on our heads. With them, we can relax, feel safe, talk openly.

A spiritual life seems impossible without friends to care for, bounce ideas off, worry about. My friendship with Jeff, I thought, demonstrated the powerful link between spirituality and the love of other people.

Though everybody needs friends, writers, like cops or

mountain climbers, *really* need friends: they are perpetually in crisis, and they spend a lot of time alone, a state in which crises loom especially large. Jeff and I grew close during a series of troubles, and our friendship deepened with each one.

When women get into trouble, I've noticed, they instinctively tend to turn outward, to their friends. Men reflexively turn inward; when they open up, it's rarely by choice.

When I first met Jeff, he was floundering, which probably explains his openness to a stranger. He was licking his wounds after a collision with Hollywood, where he and his wife, working on a screenplay, had been told for months how great they were, until suddenly they weren't told anything at all. They'd ended up broke and out of work in remote Cambridge. After months of job hunting, Michele was commuting to Boston, where she'd found work as a speechwriter. Jeff was struggling to finish a novel.

Their money was running low. Although Jeff never said so, I sensed that even a long-distance call wasn't a casual thing for him. He wasn't sure what to do with himself, stuck alone in that ancient barn of a house all week.

At the time, my own writing life was going comparatively smoothly. After six or seven years of the usual heartaches, I was a novelist and mystery writer who had published five books of fiction and was getting nice reviews, an essayist and critic who had written scores of articles for classy magazines. Thanks to the mysteries, I was a provincial celebrity, famous in a ten-block territory around my house, however unknown I was beyond that. And I had a contract to do my first nonfiction book on media and culture.

I was starting to think of myself (prematurely and fool-ishly, as it turned out) as successful, established. I had faced up to some serious problems, tackled my writing with deter-mination and energy, experienced more rejection in a few years than I'd imagined possible in a lifetime, and, like my hero the battery bunny, had kept going.

Real opportunities for friendship occur during windows, critical passages and transitions—journeys of the soul, per-haps. When you take up residence in a new place. When you have a child. When someone close to you gets sick or dies.

In the first years of my friendship with Jeff, I was going through several such shifts. So was he.

My time taking care of Emma had given the two of us a monumental gift, a close relationship that seemed a miracle, for a man. Being a dad had preoccupied, challenged, and engaged me. I wrote about it, worried about it, worked at it. It defined a decade and a half of my life.

But about the time I met Jeff, I understood that I needed some new definition to my life. I could sense a bittersweet but healthy change coming. Emma and I were beginning the long, necessary, and inevitable process of separation, a land-mark in even close relationships between parents and adoles-cent kids.

At the same time, the terrors and travails that had sent me into years of psychoanalysis had cooled a bit; I felt ready to reenter the world.

I was ripe for a brush with spirituality, burning for change. Having finally lived long enough, experienced enough, I understood that bad times were also opportunities, that good things could flow from bad and the other way around. In the same way that Buddy Holly's death had reordered my world, so had Emma's surgery. I felt raw, opened up, stirred.

IF THERE WAS an ongoing tragedy in my life—another big factor in the evolving friendship with Jeff—it was my primary family, what social scientists would call my "family of origin," in Rhode Island. Like a crashed plane, my family is a smoldering wreck, pieces of it scattered over a great distance, with many people injured and few survivors.

We had been a bitterly unhappy clan. My parents had an angry marriage that made our house tense and volatile, a place filled with wounding.

I had a much older brother, but he had moved out of the house when I was small, and our lives had evolved quite separately. We were by no means enemies, but we weren't really friends, either. He hosts a radio talk show in New England, and sometimes, before dawn, he calls to put me on the air for a few minutes to talk about some media story or other. On the air, we greet each other and ask how the other is doing; it's almost the only time we speak.

My mother, now in her late eighties, lives in an assisted-care facility, spending most of her days still struggling to come to grips with what happened to our family. She hasn't had any contact with my sister in several years.

My sister, whom I did—and do—love dearly, and to whom I'd been profoundly close as a child, had, after years of mental illness, breakdowns, addictions, and other intense suffering and treatment, entered a life in which I played absolutely no part. She had survived, a testament to her strength and courage. But we, who had talked each other to sleep when we were kids, rarely spoke as adults. She had never set foot in my house; if she were to run into Emma on the street, neither would know the other. I wasn't positive I'd know her myself.

It wasn't that we'd stopped caring for each other. It was simply that we'd seen too much together.

Hovering over this whole unhappy history was the grim visage of my father, a good and even revered man, but one of those who finds it easier to love other people's kids than his own. He acknowledged, shortly before he died, that I was not the son he'd wanted to have, and I admitted that he wasn't the father I wanted. That conversation was probably the most intimate we'd ever had.

I know my father loved me and wanted the best for me, but he also thought me a weakling and a sissy, ill prepared to survive the world. This paternal judgment is a harsh one for any son, but in many ways, he was right: I was brooding, awkward, troubled, frightened, and weird. I was bad at sports. I bred tropical fish. Well into junior high I was a bed wetter, a problem he saw as a profound character flaw.

Once a local basketball star, my father saw sports as a ticket to the best seats in life. For years he dragged me to the court and bounced basketballs off my chest or took me to a baseball diamond and hurled fastballs at my head. He screamed that I wouldn't meet the ball, couldn't make the shot, wasn't paying attention, wasn't showing heart.

Every weekend, along with otherwise pleasant spring and summer evenings, was spent in this futile struggle to make me competent at some sport—especially after I cost the local Little League a championship by letting a simple fly ball fall between my outstretched arms. I remember that long walk off the field, people in the stands booing and the other kids taunting, my father shaking his head. I knew the speech I'd get in the car home: *I told you to keep your eye on the ball.*

I was eleven when my father dragged me off to the field next to the redbrick junior high school for one of our innumerable make-me-into-a-man baseball drills. He hit a line drive that struck me in the forehead and knocked me over; as I lay in the field watching the ball roll away, I felt something shift inside me.

From what seemed a long distance away, I could hear him screaming that I should pick the ball up and try again until I got it right.

Many childhood memories are hazy to me, but this one is crystalline: I dropped my glove and walked off the field, leaving my father to hurl names after me. His shouts and insults burned into my brain. I felt an almost breathtaking fury, and clarity about what I had to do.

That would be the last such conversation he and I would ever have, I decided. I never really talked to him or listened to his advice again. And he never tried to teach me athletics after that morning, never ordered me off to a baseball field or basketball court, never mentioned what had happened. I never brought it up. I cut him off and cut myself off from him.

All of this heightened the need I felt, decades later, for something akin to family. To encounter a new friend, a near-brother, in midlife was miraculous.

Jeff and I began alternating dramas, each giving the other a chance to be a friend indeed. It was soon enough my turn to flounder. Although our friendship had begun at a point at which I considered my life comparatively, and at long last, stable, neither life nor work stays that way for long.

Emma's surgery threw Paula and me into emotional and financial turmoil. Then Jeff plunged into writing a difficult book. Some months later I had a round of fresh writing troubles. In a writer's life these bumps and bruises, I'd come to learn, weren't the exceptions but the rule. You rode them like waves, but that didn't make them less frightening.

Through all that and more, our friendship was transforming. I would never have run to the mountain without Jeff. I would never have known of the place, of course, nor would I have had the courage to go there. My nerve would have failed me a hundred times along the way. Without him, I doubt I would have survived the innumerable obstacles I would encounter once there. I certainly never dreamed that weeks after arriving, I would confront the reality that our friendship was about to change for good.

I CALLED JEFF ten times a day to strategize over the house. Should I offer more? Stay firm? Wait it out and risk having another buyer come along? Georgette sniffed a live prospect and was calling me several times a day as well. This should work, she said. You need a place to write; Lenny needs to sell the house. Remember that the house is important to him, that he is very emotional about it.

The negotiations dragged on longer than I'd thought they would and got more complicated. My initial instincts were both right and wrong: Lenny, it turned out, was seriously ill.

He *was* in the process of getting a divorce; he *did* need to sell the house. But the odd thing was, he didn't really want to sell the house at all; he loved it too much.

Still, if he were going to pass the place on to a stranger, he wanted to do it with proper ceremony. Because he was so ill, he wasn't sure if he'd be able to make it up from Long Island. But he wanted to try.

"I want to take you through it," he told me on the phone, the first time we talked. "Show you how everything works. There's a lot of things you have to know."

For a tiny little cabin, there did, in fact, seem to be many idiosyncrasies and caveats to absorb. Things about the electricity: the placement of light switches appeared unrelated to their proximity to the fixtures they operated. There were things about water and the pump. Things about winter.

The neighbors told me fond stories about the affable Lenny, who walked up and down the mountain with a flock of grumpy shar-pei dogs, some of whom kept him company on his trucking runs. Thus the long chains that graced many of the trees behind the house. Lenny wore a single earring and a long black ponytail and beard that set him apart from the other people on the mountain. But he was sweet-natured, they told me, a gentle bear.

"I love drinking up there in the winter," he told me. "I park my truck out on the road, hike in, light a fire, and keep it going for days. What the hell . . ." The house *was* well equipped for partying, with its Formica bar on the porch, cabinets full of highball and shot glasses, and all those drinking slogans and signs on the walls.

I liked Lenny and the things I'd heard about him, even if

we had vastly different tastes. I looked forward to receiving his instructions in person. But the emotional aspects of all this made Lenny more stubborn about the purchase price. While we haggled, Georgette came up with the idea of my being a tenant for July. The six-hundred-dollar rent would give Lenny some ready cash, said Georgette, and soften the impact of the price I was offering, now in the low sixties.

Of everyone, I think Georgette read the situation the best. She understood that the writer part of me wanted the house badly, and the rest of me was scared witless about buying and maintaining it. "Try writing there for one month," she said. "Rent the place and see how you feel about it then."

So in early July I pulled up to the house, my van loaded with groceries, dog food and rawhide chips, Julius and Stanley, some bedding, my computer gear, and the many, many works of Thomas Merton in paperback and hardcover. I was going to have a house on the mountain for a month, at least.

This in itself was a dream fulfilled. After years of building my life and schedule around my kid's, I pictured long, creative summers on the mountain, feeling peaceful and writerly as hell.

Jeff and Lulu came up for a few minutes to help me settle in. Lulu caught and crunched a mouse by the back door. The sun was roasting, but I assumed this was a heat wave. I was taken aback by the flies that plagued us at every step; the heat and stillness must have brought them out.

Still, we took a walk down the driveway and along the road

that splits the mountain. If the view from the house east to Vermont was spectacular, the view in the other direction was even more breathtaking. On the far crest of the mountain is an expansive meadow, perfect for dogs to walk and run through. Beyond it to the west stretched miles of valleys and farms bounded by the Adirondacks. I had not one gorgeous vista from my mountain, but two.

Jeff said he and Michele had to drive to Boston for a doctor's appointment, something to do with their trying to get pregnant. He didn't volunteer any details, and I didn't ask.

I spent two or three hours unpacking, setting up my computer, putting my clothes in the dresser. The dogs were restless, staying right by my heels. When the sun went down, it wasn't just dusk but instant night, the darkness unbroken by a neighbor's light or a familiar sound.

Our first night in the house was bleak.

Bugs poured through the holes in the screens, buzzing and biting in the dark. The house went in minutes from stifling to astonishingly cold, and I padded around in search of another blanket. Living in Lenny's house meant living with his incredible clutter: red toylike telephones, gilt-framed mirrors, and countless knickknacks. Every time I stood up I banged into a plastic yellow table or knocked askew a dried-flower wreath.

The place had the feeling of being hurriedly abandoned. Change, address books, keys, notes, and bills were lying around, as if Lenny had planned to come back for his personal things but hadn't managed to. The house hadn't been cleaned in what seemed like a long time.

Lovely as my view was, I quickly experienced its disadvantage—a brutal morning sun that burned right through the tattered window shades, inaugurating hot, airless days. Squadrons of truly ferocious bugs—those blood-sucking flies, clouds of gnats and mosquitoes, spiders, ants, and beetles climbing over and through the woodpiles, bees and no-see-ums—were our constant companions.

It was impossible to stay outside for more than a few minutes. From that first walk, I was covered with bites and welts, and Julius and Stanley kept me up half the night with their scratching. One of Julius's eyes was nearly swollen shut.

Julius and Stanley have deep reverence for life. A lot of traditional dog stuff is missing from them, just like a lot of traditional guy stuff is missing from me. They never chase squirrels. I've caught them napping in the backyard in Jersey while rabbits nibbled at seedlings in our garden two feet away. And as I saw on the mountain, neither would harm a fly—or even shake one off. So I'd swat the flies that pestered them, but there were too many to control.

Increasingly, we retreated inside, staying away from the windows and next to the fan.

At night, trying to rest in the coolness, I could hear mice skittering all over the place. What if they chewed through my computer wires or carried strange country diseases?

I called Georgette and asked for mice advice. Go see Steve at the hardware store on Main Street, she said. Or try the Agway a few blocks from there.

I wound up spending a lot of time at Steve's and at the Agway, supposedly one of a chain of farm-supply stores but, more accurately, a rural community center. All problems that aren't personal or emotional are brought to one or the other, where help is always available. Not only does the staff give more advice than Dear Abby, stopping whatever they're doing for long expositions on possible solutions, but so will all customers within earshot.

Nobody could have doubted that I was a newcomer. I pulled into the hardware store parking lot in my dusty, suburban-style minivan, suited for car pools but not for driving around a mountain. I was wearing shorts and sandals and a cap that said RE-BOOTING, accompanied by an embroidered computer. I was neither ruddy nor weathered.

Steve introduced himself and asked who I was. My house was six or seven miles from the hardware store, a long way in New Jersey but right in the neighborhood upstate.

Upstate, I identify myself in one of two ways. I am a friend of Jeff and Michele, a.k.a. "the two kids who are fixing up the old Randall place." Even better, I can say I'm a neighbor of Doc's, the retired town physician, who shares the same dirt driveway.

I couldn't believe my good fortune at actually having a neighbor called Doc. Within twenty miles of the mountain the mention of his name is a golden passport, securing good credit, fine service, and prompt attention. So I shook hands with Steve and said I lived near Doc.

"Oh, you're that writer who's renting the place next door?" Startled, I nodded.

"Georgette was in here," Steve explained. "She said I better take good care of you."

As I explained my mouse problem, four customers appeared in a semicircle. I had wondered how people here would take to strangers, but I quickly found that most of them love newcomers like me. Too dumb to know much, we are fresh ears, eager to learn of solutions, gathered over the years, for life's many challenges. Then, too, we pay money to resolve problems most locals can handle themselves.

"I got a great mouser cat," Stan, a huge man in overalls, told me. "Big cat. Be happy to let him live with you for a week. I loan him out to friends. He goes through the walls after 'em. His name is Claw."

I was tempted, but I wondered about my dogs, who were waiting out in the van. Stan walked out to take a look. I opened the back door, and once Stan was thoroughly licked and slobbered over, he and I agreed that a sleepover with Claw might not be so great an idea.

Another man said he'd built a cheap wooden trap, something like a lobster trap, and stuck old cheese in it. Once mice venture in, he gets his shotgun, he said, winking, and the mice succumb to "lead poisoning."

Stan chuckled. "A lot of my raccoons die from that."

Various traps and baits were proposed and debated. "My daughter wanted me to get one of those humane traps," said another customer. Everybody's eyes rolled. Daughters. What did they know of the world? I was enjoying this bizarre conversation; I was one of the guys, accepted, worthy of counseling. Even to be offered Claw seemed a compliment.

Steve, noticing the growing clot of customers, finally stepped in, handing me some plastic mousetraps. "Peanut butter," he said firmly. "Peanut butter will get them every time."

Feeling a bit on the handy side, I bought a half dozen traps from the highly credible Steve, launching a daily massacre.

Perhaps because they are willful, or perhaps because they'd lived relatively unmolested for a couple of years, the mice on my mountain seemed reluctant to grasp the new reality of my presence.

We engaged in furious combat from the first day.

They came in waves, like creatures in a Hitchcock movie. I heard them skittering around at night. They nibbled on the dog-food bag, left droppings in the kitchen. One fell into the toilet bowl and drowned. They became the first symbol of my struggle to reclaim Lenny's house and make it mine. If I was staying, or even thinking of staying, then the mice were going, preferably before Paula came up for her first look at my new folly.

The traps Steve had recommended were supposed to be lethal. "You put the peanut butter on this end," he'd explained, clicking one open. "A mouse comes in"—he paused dramatically as the trap snapped shut—"and they die. Then you take 'em outside and flip 'em into the woods like this." He flicked his wrist, and the trap opened a hair. I could picture the offending mouse whizzing through the air.

Alas, the traps he had demonstrated so effortlessly seemed impossibly complex Rube Goldberg contraptions to me. When I opened one, it would snap shut, popping into the air or onto the floor. If I managed to hold it open briefly, then the act of baiting it would trigger the mechanism, snapping it shut again, spewing peanut butter onto the shag carpeting.

The first casualty of the traps was, appropriately, Stanley, who'd been enjoying the rain of peanut butter. I had carefully opened a trap and managed to gently smear some peanut butter on it. But when I turned away for a moment, I heard a piteous yelp. The trap had snapped on Stanley's exploratory nose.

"If you were any kind of a dog," I yelled, "you'd catch the damned mice yourself. Watch your ass, or I'll get Claw in here." Even better, I thought, maybe Lulu could visit for a few days. There wouldn't be a rodent left alive on the mountain.

It took most of an hour to get the first traps loaded, primed, and transported into the basement. But I persevered. And the next morning, as the sun streamed onto the mountain, I crept into the basement, flashlight in hand.

There were three dead mice, small and brown, with white chests. I felt no revulsion at this, the deadly but necessary work of the hunter. I picked the traps up and, with dead mice hanging from each, headed out into the backyard.

Flipping them into the woods didn't work for me, though. I flicked my wrist, as Steve had taught me, but the mouse bounced off my leg and landed on my shoe.

Stanley tried to sniff one, then backed off in disgust. Julius, as always, watched me curiously, too dignified to lick peanut butter from a mousetrap, too picky to eat a mouse. In fact, because of his delicate stomach, Julius ate only hypoallergenic vegetarian dog food. The guys at the Agway would get a charge out of *that*. I decided this would be our little secret.

After a few days, there were dead mice scattered all around the back of the house. Georgette, dropping by to check on me,

administered a scolding. This wouldn't do, she said. It would
only attract other rodents and God knows what else. I went
around with a garbage bag and pliers to collect the corpses.

I was still killing mice weeks later. I had stumbled across
world mouse headquarters. It dawned on me that this was
going to be a long battle. The enemy would never run out of
soldiers dedicated to occupying my house, but I, making up
in stubbornness what I lacked in hunting skills, would never
surrender.

Meanwhile, on other fronts, the rented cabin began to
fray from unaccustomed daily use. Light bulbs in ancient fixtures and cockeyed lamps began to blow out. Faucets came
off in my hands. Holes appeared in screens. Handles came
off drawers. Bug carcasses lined the windowsills.

I had trouble making long-distance phone calls. Every
time I dialed home, an operator came on and took my number. When I set up my PowerBook, the operator's interruptions meant I couldn't dial up to the Internet. After several
days, I realized that something was wrong and called Bell
Atlantic.

The service rep could barely keep from laughing.

"Don't you know?" she said. "You're on a four-way party
line."

Party line? I hadn't even heard the term for years, outside
old black-and-white movies. But of course—the operator
came on so that the phone company would know which of
the sharing parties to bill.

I had to be able to make direct long-distance calls, I
explained. I needed a private line. And I had to be able to get

on the Net, as I wrote a column for a Web site, so I needed a dedicated computer line.

The service rep was friendly but firm. "That will take weeks, probably a month. And it will cost you a few hundred dollars." Great. A contributing editor for *Wired* magazine, a columnist for its Web site, "Hotwired," was on a mountaintop, unplugged and out of business.

I struggled for several days to get comfortable, buying another fan, setting up a makeshift desk in one of the bedrooms. But it remained boiling until midday. I took to driving down to Jeff's to plug in my computer, check my E-mail, do some work. Down in the valley, his house was shaded and cool; there were fewer bugs.

This whole thing was a mistake, I began to think. I missed my wife and kid. I called Paula and told her how discouraging it all was, how unpleasant it would be to write here for even a month, how much work and money it would take to fix the house up after that. "Good," she said. "Pack up the stuff, put the dogs in the van, and come home. Let's write it off as a six-hundred-dollar mistake instead of a seventy-thousand-dollar disaster."

She had gone from resignation to relief.

I knew as well as she did that we couldn't really afford this place, that we weren't embarking on this project as an enthusiastic couple, the way most married people buy second homes, that this wasn't a reasoned or timely decision. Why wasn't she raising hell?

Because she's unusual. Because she's so comfortable with herself that she has no great need to control others. Because she's so fiercely independent that she understands and reveres independence.

Perhaps for the same reason that I wouldn't have stopped her, had the shoe been on the other foot. She wanted me to have what I needed, and she knew that I needed something badly, even if neither of us could say precisely what that was.

Though other people were more skeptical.

I'd been hearing the questions, seeing the dubious looks and raised eyebrows from the first. How could I leave my family for weeks on end? What was really going on? A friend I'd met on the street put her arm on my shoulder and asked if it were true that Paula and I were separating. I was surprised at the number of people who insisted that this kind of freedom wouldn't be possible in their own marriages, that they wouldn't dare it and their spouses would never permit it.

The fact is, running to the mountain *was* hard. Don't try this at home, I told an old friend; it isn't for everybody. The separation was often painful. It's no small thing to have a strong marriage or a great kid, or to leave them behind. Whenever I headed for the mountain over the next few months, the farewells went on for ten or fifteen minutes, extended by fussing and repacking, hugs for Emma and Paula, and trips back to retrieve things I always seemed to forget. I called on the cell phone from the New York State Thruway. I called home as soon as I arrived.

Still, I wanted to go, and it didn't seem to have occurred to Paula to object. "You're supposed to be upset," I kept telling her. "Why aren't you?"

Usually she just shrugged or laughed.

When I first told my father that Paula and I wanted to be married, he cautioned me against it. She was an exotic, threatening creature to him, a feminist who planned to work and insisted on keeping her own name.

I remember telling him that I thought feminism was like a train—you could either get out of the way or get run over, but you couldn't stop it. It wasn't just that women would be liberated, I told him, but that I would.

He was unconvinced, but I was right. I was freer than some men because my wife believed that each of us should be able to pursue what was important to us. This belief was affirmed every time I headed north.

At times, I could see that she missed me. Once in a while she even told me so, or cursed me good-naturedly for sticking her with all the chores—driving Emma to lessons and friends' houses, shopping, cooking, cat care—that I usually handled. At least Emma no longer required that exhausting, minute-by-minute attention that had so consumed us years ago when she was little.

At other points, when it got particularly lonely up there, I'd call Paula four or five times a day and exasperate her.

"Didn't we just talk two hours ago?" she'd say, busy with her work. "What's the matter?"

The truth was that our marriage and our family were not affected dramatically by distance, something it was important for me to learn. The three of us were close when I went, and we remained close while I was there. Paula would never understand why anyone was making a big deal of this. She pointed out that the laundry load was significantly reduced by my absence, and she got a lot more work done.

But at the moment, my decision to bail out was welcome news at home.

Then I called Jeff, back from Boston, and told him my decision. He suggested we go out to eat and talk. In Manchester we had dinner at the Quality Restaurant, a place Norman Rockwell had appropriated for one of his paintings, *War News*. I remember eating chilled blueberry soup.

I told Jeff I'd had it. Even if Lenny agreed to my bargain-basement price, the place was a wreck. It needed much more work and resources than someone like me could possibly undertake. How wise I was to have rented it first.

Jeff disagreed. "This is a great house. It won't take much to fix it up. You could expand the porch; labor is cheap up here. Meanwhile, you can get a window air conditioner if you want to work inside. The flies will be gone by August. You need a place to write. Just give it some time, a couple more weeks. You've already paid for the month."

This made sense. Or maybe it was just what I wanted to hear. Jeff was, after all, my Natty Bumppo, a guide wise in the ways of such things. I called Paula back and told her I was going to wait before deciding. She sighed.

It's a scary thing to negotiate unexplored territory without your faithful guide.

Jeff is twelve years younger, but because we share so many interests—books, movies, the Web, media, writing, humor, hiking, family history, love of dogs—it had never quite occurred to me we weren't the same age.

He and Michele had talked occasionally about wanting to

have kids, and when they hadn't conceived they began exploring it more seriously, but I had assumed they were still considering it. Then, the very week I moved into the house, Michele and Jeff went to Boston to undergo in vitro fertilization.

I didn't think about it much at the time; perhaps I didn't want to know about it. I was just emerging from my intense parenting period, and Paula and I were both looking forward to life beyond car pools. In my mind, my future included lots of long country walks with Jeff and our dogs.

Besides, Jeff and Michele seemed so happy. They both worked hard, but their days were also full of a country kind of leisure completely alien to me. They spent hours planning and cooking meals for friends, which involved driving to Vermont for fish, picking vegetables and herbs from their garden, debating the choice of wines. Afterward, meals were analyzed in painstaking detail. How was the salad? Was the meat cooked properly? Did the sauce work?

Where movie theaters and other amusements are miles away, cooking for friends takes on a distinct meaning, especially during the bitter winters. Entertaining and reciprocating assumed an importance I'd never encountered outside of Jane Austen.

Evenings and weekends, Jeff and Michele were often in Michele's beautiful, elaborate garden, watering, thinning, weeding, fertilizing. Having kids seemed almost antithetical to this picture.

So I was amazed to learn, shortly after moving into my rented retreat, that Michele was pregnant. And having trouble. She began experiencing severe abdominal pains and

bleeding and was admitted to a Boston hospital. Jeff was terrified. And he was gone.

It was jarring, abrupt. Every morning I went to Jeff's
empty house to bring in the mail, let the cat out, water the
garden. Every evening I went back to let the cat in. Jeff called
me as often as he could with worried updates. With him
away, my house seemed even uglier and lonelier.

Over the next few days, as Michele stabilized, Jeff
returned to do some work. But both of us were in shock. He
seemed not to have really expected to have a baby or thought
through the implications. He looked as if he'd been walloped
with a two-by-four.

As a well-known, voluble fan of parenthood, I was happy
for them, I really was. But the news was a stunner to me, too.

I think it drove home to me for the first time that Jeff and
I weren't quite peers, after all. He was starting a family, a
monumental turning point in life. I had to acknowledge that
my child-rearing years, from which I had derived so much
love, identity, and engagement—not to mention articles and
books—were ending soon. I might never know Jeff's child as
an adult, a jarring idea that brought home, again, the implications of turning fifty.

How had I missed this enormous divergence in our lives?

Along with happiness for him, I felt real sadness, something almost akin to grief. People without kids, naturally, can
hardly begin to imagine how different life with small children
is. If Jeff were going to be a loving and attentive father—there
was no question that he would—then our friendship would
alter, perhaps fade. I could see more clearly than he could how
much it would change, because I'd been where he was going.

How much time would Jeff have over the next few years for leisurely hikes in Vermont? To swim with the dogs in the Battenkill? How many nights would we spend sitting up yakking about our lives, our families, our writing pains?

I'd lost close friends this way before, even abandoned a couple myself. When men are pressed, their friendships go to the bottom of the list. I knew, of course, that we would still be close. He would need me, and I intended to be there, to fight for this friendship, not let it slide away. But it wouldn't be the same. This journey to the mountain suddenly took on a different cast.

Early the next morning I sat out on the mountain, in the same spot Jeff and I had had lunch a while earlier. I watched the sun stream across the valley, feeling like I'd just lost my best chum. An old loneliness, familiar, almost comfortable, settled over me.

I'd discovered a half-hour window between the first sunlight and the ascent of the bloodsucking flies. In those minutes, I could take a cup of coffee outside, give the dogs some rawhide chews, and plan the day ahead. Soon the sun would launch its morning assault and the flies would amass, and we would retreat, pausing only to collect the rodent casualties from the previous night.

I decided that the mice, the flies, and the sun were all in it together, conspiring to punish me for thinking that life could be so simple, that I could have such a good pal and keep him, that I could find such a lovely spot to write and claim it. I saw my spiritual summer burning off in the morning mists, along with my friendship.

I was surprised to hear a car in the driveway this early. The dogs barked in a perfunctory way, as a man came around to where I was sitting and offered his hand. He was a neighbor, he said, and a friend of Lenny's. He wanted to let me know that Lenny wouldn't be coming up to give me a tour of the house after all. He wanted to let me know that Lenny was very sick. He suggested, without exactly saying so, that Lenny might not live very long. That I might want to close on the house soon, if I wanted it.

He shook hands again and drove off the mountain. I felt a shiver. Poor Lenny. He'd never even get to say good-bye to this house. And these weren't exactly the circumstances under which I hoped to buy it.

I checked the mousetraps, a grisly ritual now incorporated into my days. I pulled open the steel doors to the basement. The dogs sat on the top steps, gazing down and wagging as, using a flashlight, I looked for the traps I'd set the night before. Just one small brown corpse today.

Steve assures me the traps are humane, that death is swift and certain. After weeks of carnage, I'm not so sure. But I did have a much needed victory that morning: when I flicked my trap the way Steve had shown me, the mouse went flying twenty feet into the woods.

"Aha, boys," I exulted to the dogs, "smooth as glass."

A few moments later we were finishing our coffee and rawhide. The flies were beginning to swarm. I addressed the dogs like a general preparing his troops for combat. "It's just us, guys. You, me, a billion flies, and about ten thousand mice. Otherwise, we are all alone."

SOLITUDE

*This silence confirms my solitude. The more I am
in it, the more I love it. One day it will possess me
entirely and no man will ever see me again.*

—THOMAS MERTON, *TURNING TOWARD THE WORLD*

WHEN I GREW up, I was mostly alone. And after writing for more than a decade, I'm accustomed to quiet. But the quiet of life in New Jersey isn't like the quiet on the mountaintop. At home I hear planes, cars, trains, sirens. Kids yell, dogs bark, lawn mowers roar. Sometimes, after a rain, I can hear water running through the storm sewers.

Inside my basement office, my computer hums. The pipes in the house groan and clatter. Phones or faxes are always ringing or beeping. Looking out my window, I can see ten or twenty houses, all within easy shouting distance. On spring nights, when windows are open, I can smell other people's dinners as I walk with the dogs, hear husbands and wives fighting, listen to them order their kids to bed, see the lights from computer screens and TV's flickering.

I'd never experienced the kind of quiet that hit me like a sledgehammer on the mountaintop. It was as if all the rest of my life had been sucked down a huge black hole, leaving only me and the dogs.

When the sun sank, the silence hastened up the valley to the mountaintop like an onrushing ghost. In the daytime, there was an occasional sound—tractors, trucks on the mountain road, the distant rumble of tires on a wet highway, birdsong and insects' hum. But at night, there was absolute silence and, except for the occasional headlight slicing through the valley, no light. If the moon wasn't out, I was immersed in blackness, like floating in a pool of ink. I couldn't see another house, hear a voice. I really could hear myself think.

Tonight I called Paula, who was off on assignment for *The Washington Post,* where she works as a reporter, but she'd checked out of her hotel. I wrote a letter to Emma, away on an overseas service project, to tell her about the birds, the valley, the morning mists. But it would be weeks before she got it, and she'd probably find it strange that her father, the pallid movie-loving basement dweller, was prattling on about wildlife. I could picture her eyes rolling.

I had been reading my Merton books, especially his writing about solitude and silence; it wasn't comforting. Beware of solitude, he warned, it's not something to play with. "It is deadly serious, and much as I have wanted it, I have not been serious enough about it. It is not enough just to 'like solitude' or love it even. Even if you like it, solitude can wreck you, I believe, if you desire it only for your own sake."

This was daunting because I did desire it for my own sake, not in the service of religion or God. I wanted solitude for me, and if Merton was right, I'd leave the mountain in much worse shape than I'd arrived.

ON THE MOUNTAIN, I found myself truly, literally alone for perhaps the first time in my life—solitude being very different from loneliness—without really being prepared or knowing how to respond. Like Merton, I'd left the real world, though temporarily.

After a week or two in residence, I'd agreed to buy the Last Resort and its 2.5 surrounding acres, pending various contingencies and inspections. I don't quite know what tipped me over the edge; I suppose I meant to buy the house all along. In the end, Lenny and I, prodded by Georgette and by his need to conclude the deal quickly, wound up splitting the difference: he came down in his price, I came up, and we settled on $67,500. Some Jaguars cost more.

Meanwhile, I remained a tenant, until the closing sometime in August.

Spiritual seekers often go off on their own, withdraw to monasteries and retreats, meditate for hours. Like Merton, they seek to draw close to God. Or, like Henry David Thoreau, they decide to see what they are made of. Or, like Nelson Mandela or Mahatma Gandhi, they fortify themselves in solitude for the struggles they will undertake. Solitude seems not to break or isolate them but to provide insight, courage, and clarity.

Yet solitude frightened and intimidated me. I knew it would be difficult and complicated, and I didn't think I had the sustaining conviction, faith, strength, or purpose of those spiritual heavyweights.

But neither did I want to shut myself out of these explorations because of the towering people associated with them. I didn't want only to read about other people's trips; I wanted to take my own.

The fortitude required here was oddly contemporary. I wasn't risking life and limb as Gandhi had or making the enormous personal sacrifices of Merton. The greatest perils I faced were the judgments of peers and contemporaries, ridicule, and futility. What if I spent all that time alone but learned and accomplished nothing? Small dangers, but powerful in their ability to stop a seeker cold.

But this was always an obstacle to quests, spirituality, and change—thinking they were the exclusive province of the larger-than-life. I was desperate for solitude, for the time and space to hear myself think and thus do a better job of it.

As such notions—solitude, spirituality—have been made to seem godly, they appear to float high above our mundane and unheroic experiences. Working for long hours for big companies, rushing kids around to malls and soccer games, squirreling money away for college and retirement, we want to read about conversations with God but don't really expect to have any ourselves.

All this loftiness leaves many of us, especially those of us stranded for one reason or another outside the cozy confines of organized religion, feeling like spiritual voyeurs, scavengers of other people's wisdom.

My hope, coming to the mountain, was that change, spirituality, and idealism aren't only way Up There but also Down Here, in the details of daily life—family, work, friends, dogs, dreams.

Merton did his best to live in a vacuum, fighting to move into a hermitage where he could practice his ideals freely and fully. Even living by himself in a cabin in the woods, he rarely was left alone long enough to do so. What chance do the rest of us have? We have to weave our spirituality and idealism into everyday tasks and obligations, if we are to know them at all.

That's the job I'd come to do. This wasn't a vacation house. It was a workplace.

Tonight I needed to get down to business, stay out in the dark, not go inside to curl up in the soft yellow chair, turn on the CD player, and read. I needed to face solitude from the outset, and convince myself that I could, so that I wouldn't have to face it again and again.

LOOKING OUT THE kitchen window after a monkish supper—some sugar snap peas, a fresh peach, whole wheat bread with a slice of cheese—I saw the last streaks of reddish light vanish from the sky.

In the quiet, I could feel old terrors welling up, kid stuff, buried deep by the rush of life and routine, not felt for years yet all too familiar. As quiet as the mountaintop and woods are, I wasn't afraid of what was out there. I was afraid of what's inside of me, of what will come in these long nights.

So I got ready. I fortified myself. I hadn't been much of a drinker for years, but I'd brought a bottle of twelve-year Scotch purchased back in New Jersey. It was good stuff, Glenlivet, thirty-six dollars a bottle.

I threw two ice cubes in a glass and took the bottle outside, christening the mountain with a splash onto the grass. I toasted Lenny for building this house. I wished Jeff and Michele good luck in having their baby. I toasted Julius and Stanley and thanked them for their faithful companionship. I sent love beams to Paula and Emma, wherever they were. I wished myself good luck in acquiring this odd place and in working well here.

Then I gulped the Glenlivet down, like a patient awaiting surgery and desperate for anesthesia. The old familiar burning started deep and spread outward. I took a deep breath.

Come and get me.

Like me, or perhaps because of me, the dogs were skittish. This kind of isolation was new to them, too, though they could probably hear many more things than I could.

As I settled in an Adirondack chair nursing the Scotch, Julius put his head on my knee and Stanley leaned against my other leg. Anything that came after one of us would have to contend with all of us, formidable in mass if lacking ferocity.

It was sticky, hot, and still. Things fluttered overhead. Bats, I suspected. Bugs swarmed around the yellow light at the side of the house.

The stars were brighter and thicker than I'd ever seen them. I thought I glimpsed a shooting star or two. But even when I saw them, I couldn't believe it, writing them off as jets or tricks my eyes were playing. Jeff says the fast-moving lights were satellites.

I poured myself a second drink, gave each of the dogs a biscuit. Their familiar, industrious chomping was a soothing sound. I felt a rising dread nonetheless.

. . .

THE SPIRIT OF Merton would help fortify me, along with the Glenlivet. He stood his ground, toughed it out, hung on. So would I.

I'd always been taken by Merton's idealism, by the impassioned young man setting off in the dark to vanish behind the monastery walls and seek God. As his letters and diaries showed, idealism was rough to sustain at fifty.

Yet Merton retained a nearly childlike sense of faith and innocence to the end—his loneliness, his struggles with ecclesiastic authority, his longing for whiskey, and a doomed love affair all notwithstanding.

Aware of the dangers of narcissism and the potential for ridicule, he never quit on the process. October 1965: "There has been much self-searching, some futile, some disquieting. It may be excessive, but there is something in the core of my being that needs to be revealed. I wonder if I can face it. Is it futile to even try?" Aware of the potential for ridicule and the dangers of narcissism myself, I felt especially close to Merton in the dark, despite my unease. It had to do with coming to this shag-carpeted hermitage.

Maybe it was that Merton never took a straight path anywhere. Merton was a holy man but no saint. He was very much a human being with his fair share, perhaps more, of frailties. Perhaps that's what always made him seem so accessible.

Merton, writes one biographer, was a restless monk. On the one hand, he bristled at the lack of solitude in his life; on the other, he raged about restrictions on his travel. He craved isolation, yet basked in celebrity. He fantasized about the lonely life of the hermit, while cranking out a stream of letters to the famous and influential. He preached obedience and humility but battled his abbot for decades. He chafed at the censorship to which his writings were subjected and often thought about leaving both the monastery and his religious order.

He was nearly consumed by the ferocious conflict between the seeker he wanted to be and the human he was, a man who could be intemperate and intolerant, who in his youth loved sex and alcohol and impregnated a lover, who later took a vow of chastity and then, at the age of fifty-one, fell in love.

Merton was twenty-two, a Columbia University graduate student, when he began his conversion to Catholicism and experienced the first of a series of profound callings to religious life. He chanced to walk into a Manhattan church— Corpus Christi on 121st Street—and found what I'd always wanted to find, what most of us, I think, want to find. No one, he wrote of that momentous day, can find faith simply by wanting to. He must receive grace, an "actual light and impulsion of the mind."

Merton described his leisurely walk down Broadway in the sunlight afterward, looking about at a changed landscape. He could not understand what had happened to make him so at peace. "All I know is that I walked in a new world. Even the ugly buildings of Columbia were transfigured in it, and everywhere was peace in these streets designed for violence and noise. Sitting outside the gloomy little Childs restaurant at 111th Street, behind the dirty, boxed bushes, and eating breakfast, was like sitting in the Elysian Fields."

Even as I knew that that kind of faith was forever out of my reach, I wished I could have found the same impulse, with the same joy.

Two days after the Pearl Harbor bombing, when he was twenty-six, Merton entered the Trappist monastery in Gethsemani. He should have vanished from the outside world at that point, but as called to write as he was to pray, he published *The Seven Storey Mountain* in 1948, an instant bestseller, which made him the most famous monk in the world, a celebrity for the rest of his life.

One of his journal entries kept nagging at me. He wrote it when he was more or less the age I am, plagued with physical problems and seeing himself as beginning to be old. It marked the fourteenth anniversary of his ordination.

He wished, he wrote sadly, that he could say his years in the priesthood had been years of "ever-growing fulfillment and order and integration." Instead, "I realize more and more the depth of my frustration and the apparent finality of my defeat." He was worn down, he wrote, easily discouraged. "The depressions are deeper, more frequent. I am near fifty. People think I am happy."

They did. I knew because I was one of them. The bestselling Merton was a joyous monk, who told in *The Seven Storey Mountain* of nearly weeping in happiness as he chanted the Magnificat with his fellow monastic souls.

The Merton who looked back on his lonely life and saw defeat and failure, who was a prisoner of his own beautiful, prolific prose, wrote on one of the first days alone in his hermitage of weeping piteously at the sight of a wounded deer. It was clear that he was weeping as much for himself as for the poor creature. In his story, the deer miraculously bounds away, seemingly in perfect health. But where could Merton go?

Much as I'd wanted him to guide and strengthen me on this trip—counted on it, in fact—we were utterly different. I had planned to lean on him; instead, I found myself stuck mostly with me.

He chose to be a monk in order to be a holy man, and I had chosen to try to be a better man without being a monk.

He chose not only solitude but loneliness, and I have chosen family and friends.

He left the world behind, the better to seek God, and I had left God behind, the better to deal with the world.

UNLIKE MERTON, OF course, I could back off anytime, go inside or return to Jersey. I noticed that I kept looking out at my van, as if to make sure it was still there. It would only take half an hour to throw my things together and head toward the New York State Thruway.

I wouldn't have to ever come back. Other than Georgette, there'd be nobody to even say good-bye to. Lenny could have the rental money for July and then put the house back on the market. Jeff and I would resume the earlier pattern of our friendship—telephone calls, occasional visits. My wife would be relieved, even delighted.

But there was a bigger choice here, I knew. If idealism

really was pursuing one's dreams, then I wanted to try it. Idealists were unhip, out of style at the moment, on the fringes. But they hung on. They persisted. They kept looking.

I thought silence was the fuel with which I could sustain myself; it nourished the soul, fed the dreams. Merton was right: silence was powerful, medicinal stuff, whether you were looking for God or a way to survive your boss for another week. And if silence was the fuel, change was the means.

There are times in one's life, those key moments Merton called journeys of the soul, that I might more prosaically call passages—marriage, divorce, children, moving, illness, workplace crises and challenges, the prospect of friendship, moral dramas, and spiritual decisions—when one simply has to stop, step out of one's routine, and take the trouble to think. It's not a luxury but an obligation: how else to even try to make measured, considered decisions based on deliberation and self-awareness rather than on impulse or fear?

Going to a monastery is one way to think these passages through, and running to a mountain another, but so is taking a long walk with a dog, driving to the nearest beach, or, failing all that, waking up before dawn to sit in a quiet room for an hour to consider the course of your life.

On the mountaintop, I came to see my own life in a deeper, richer, and more useful way than I'd been able to do elsewhere. But I would learn that stepping outside oneself was a matter less of geography than of state of mind.

I poured another drink, then looked at the bottle. It was emptying quickly.

I didn't want to take up drinking regularly here. At times

in my past, I drank too much. I already had a sense of how dangerous that could be during the mythically brutal winters. I'd heard too many stories about subzero weather, blocked roads, howling winds, four-foot snowdrifts, and afternoons that slipped into icy blackness at three o'clock.

Besides, I couldn't afford a drinking problem, not at the price of Glenlivet.

I DOZED OFF until something woke me, and I sat upright in the wooden chair. Behind me the bedroom shades were backlit, and the house looked inviting. My back and legs felt stiff, and I was cold. Across the valley, a half-moon hung over the mountain so that even in the darkness I could see its ridges and valleys. My watch said 4:00 A.M.

My dogs, faithful as ever, sat right where I'd last seen them. Julius, I saw as my eyes got used to the dark, was watching me; probably he'd been keeping vigil all night. Stanley, more trusting and oblivious, was snoring.

I wondered, out of courtesy and curiosity, whether Lenny had ever sat here with his shar-peis. I decided to write Lenny a note, if our deal went through, to tell him I loved his house, would take great care of it, and would never turn the hot water on before the cold, as he'd instructed me on the phone. I felt uneasy about dissing his house so much, calling it a wreck, laughing about the dumb signs, the slimy pool and ugly paintings. Sitting here in the dark, it seemed a bulwark, a castle.

As time floated by unmeasured and the sky grayed, I found I wasn't thinking about much of anything at all. I was somewhere between drowsiness, contemplation, and peace. My mind, always racing, stopped hopscotching. I wasn't worrying about my family or thinking about my next work project; I wasn't anxious about the coming building and sewage inspections, the lack of phone lines, or the ghost of the man who used to be here.

Bit by bit, perhaps overwhelmed by all the beauty and quiet on every side, I let those subjects pass. My daughter was fine; I didn't have to feel guilty about being away from her. Paula would come to love this house. There was, at this moment, nothing to worry about.

Let go, I kept telling myself.

Looking up at the clouds, I tried to imagine my sister's face. I had to guess at it. It had been nearly five years since I'd last seen her, at my father's funeral. She'd told me then that she would never come to another family gathering, and I knew she was always as good as her word.

I was groggy, mildly buzzed, but not, I think, drunk. I spoke aloud to see if my speech was slurred. "Hey, Jane." The words sounded fine. The dogs, startled, jumped to their feet, alert, ready. They looked at each other, then at me, but no clues were forthcoming.

Of course I was talking to Jane. That made perfect sense. There was always Jane, a friend in the night. Whenever there was quiet and emptiness, there was Jane, solitude's sister as well as mine.

We lost Jane around the time I was nine or ten. I remember her breaking down quite distinctly. The two of us were in the basement of our house, playing a board game, when she simply, suddenly, fell apart. She began screaming that our parents hated her, weeping uncontrollably, wringing her hands. I was shocked beyond speech.

Jane and I were the closest of friends, together day and night, allies against our volatile parents. We comforted each other, took each other's punishments, lied for each other. We were siblings in arms, facing the dangerous and irrational forces arrayed against us.

Two years older than I, she was our leader, strategist, and seer. It was she who'd figured out that we could talk past our bedtimes as long as the TV was on. She knew how to convincingly fake sleep. She knew the histrionics that won sympathy, the guilt-inducing tricks that warded off punishment.

Now she had turned our little kingdom inside out. She had abruptly collapsed, turned into some other person, babbling, crying, outside herself. Had I missed something, signs I should have seen?

From that day, our family life was a nightmare without end. My sister was never really well again. She locked herself in her room, railing against my parents, breaking dishes, refusing to agree to any rules. She dressed strangely, ate odd things at strange times, cried for hours. She refused to see her friends, attend family functions, celebrate holidays.

Later, rebelling in every conceivable self-destructive way, she developed a series of addictions, to cigarettes, drugs, alcohol. Her teeth turned black and her hair fell out. Married and divorced, she had two children sometimes reduced to begging neighbors in their apartment building for food. We never talked much again.

My father, a social worker showered with community awards for his admirable work with children, regarded my sister as his great shame, an awful secret to be kept at all costs. He couldn't handle having so troubled a kid. And my mother couldn't deal with the inevitable finger-wagging mental illness evoked at the time—was it her fault? So my parents hid my sister's troubles from the members of their temple, from the rabbi, from their closest friends and relatives.

Their decision sealed our fate as a family, doomed my sister to a lifetime of pain and struggle, ended any prospect of normalcy. There was never again one day of fun in our home, just unrelenting anger and fear. Jane's troubles became the central drama of all our lives then and, in some ways, for good.

The sibling who watches, I've learned, falls apart too, in different ways. I couldn't bear it. It became my mission to get her help, which led to long years of struggle with my parents, a conflict we never resolved and from which we never emerged, one that cemented for good my fury at my father.

She didn't need help, he told me a thousand times. We wouldn't go outside the family. He was a social worker; if she needed help, he'd do it himself. He never wavered, reconsidered, agonized, or doubted.

On the mountain, lubricated with Glenlivet, I was awash with regret, remembering how utterly I'd failed her. I fought with my father and badgered my mother, demanding they get help for Jane. I threatened to call the police and once even did. I visited our rabbi, called my uncle. I begged my grandparents, neither of whom could speak much English. I went to talk to the parish priest at a church down the block. No one could or would help us.

Meanwhile, my sister became a ghost. She vanished from the world, an invisible person who ceased to exist outside our house. People whispered about her.

My father, I think, wanted her out of the house, which is why he was so adamant that she go off to college, very much against common sense and her own will. She was in a dreadful state, and higher education proved every bit the catastrophe it promised to be. She finally left our house for good, swallowed up in the eddies of the sixties.

It was out of this mayhem, I think, that I received the great gift of dreaming while crying myself to sleep, trying to soothe myself with fantasies and stories. As a writer, I sometimes wished there was a market for the rich stories that danced eternally inside my head.

The image I pictured now wasn't that of the child I felt close to but that of the middle-aged woman I hardly knew. She was wearing her old knowing smile, though she said nothing. She wasn't a ghost or a spirit, just a picture I'd conjured up.

Soon afterward, the sky grew lighter, as if by some secret and prearranged signal, and the woods around the house exploded in birdsong. My sister slipped away from my mind again, and I could no longer summon her face.

THE SUN POURED over the mountaintop, forcing me up; the flies would soon be on the move. The woods were alive with birds, hopping from tree to tree. A cloud sailed past the mountain across the valley and became impaled on it.

A hummingbird zoomed out of the woods and toward me like a dive-bomber. I had a churning stomach and a pounding headache.

Out there on the mountaintop at the beginning of the day, I was drained but excited.

Maybe this elaborate, spur-of-the-moment trip was just a new way to be lost. Perhaps I wanted so badly for there to be meaning and revelation at fifty that I'd decided to run to a mountaintop to make it so.

Maybe it was something more, something daring and rewarding. Maybe the key to living the rest of my life was up here. I couldn't wait to find out, either way.

So why envision my poor sister? Is this what came of solitude, old demons and torments bubbling up at will? I thought that her appearance was a signal, telling me it was okay to be here.

I'd been lucky; I'd remained intact enough to have some dreams to chase. This mountaintop aerie was such a dream.

Too busy surviving, Jane had never known that luxury; she was robbed of one of the greatest of human gifts. In a sense, she took the heat for both of us and, in so doing, saved my hide. I had maneuvering room, time alone. I became a master at slipping out of sight, finding nooks and spaces in which to brood and, thus, to escape.

It was years, decades, before it dawned on me that some of my fantasies were realizable. For thirty years I had dreamed of writing, until my psychiatrist stunned me one morning by asking why I wasn't doing it.

I thought she was mad. To work by myself spinning stories

was a little like John Wayne leading a cavalry charge—something every boy daydreams about but never thinks for a second he could actually do.

Out of analysis, my first profoundly spiritual experience, I came to understand that dreams, hope, and faith were inextricably linked. That it was critical to have and pursue dreams and to believe that they can sometimes materialize. But that their pursuit often requires enormous amounts of both hope and faith.

For years I'd had the dreams, but hope and faith were harder to come by. Perhaps the most critical task for me here on the mountain was to strengthen this part of myself. If the remaining years of my life were to be meaningful and challenging, I would need new dreams, and I'd also have to develop the necessary hope to believe they could come to pass, along with the faith required to achieve them.

It was precisely this hope and faith that my sister had been deprived of. I feared she only wanted peace, and however entitled she was to that, it broke my heart.

The last time we talked, almost a year ago, I'd told her once again that I knew what she had suffered and would never stop being sorry for it. "Look," she had said. "I know you tried to help me. I really know. Go be happy. One of us should be."

Now the phone rang. Georgette was calling to remind me about the next day's round of appointments. The reality check, jolting me from then to now, forcing me to span nearly four decades in a few seconds, was disorienting. I had to remind myself where I was, what Georgette was talking about. She'd called to bring me back to earth.

"I'll be there first thing, with lots of company. Have the coffeepot going," she instructed. "Joe Bates is coming to look at the septic system at nine. An architect's inspecting the house at nine-thirty. Exterminator at ten. And we have to take a water sample to send off to the state lab for testing. Have your checkbook ready."

Humbled on the Mountain

As animals go, even in so limited a space as our world, man is botched and ridiculous. Few other brutes are so stupid and so cowardly. The commonest yellow dog has far sharper senses and is infinitely more courageous, not to say more honest and dependable. The ants and the bees are, in many ways, far more intelligent and ingenious; they manage their government with vastly less quarreling, wastefulness and imbecility.

—H. L. Mencken, "Man's Place in Nature"

LOTS OF CARS were more expensive than my house on the mountaintop. But buying a house was more complicated than buying a car. I had to sign a form promising that I would research my title, pay off any taxes, never complain about farming smells. I had to disclose my income and declare my debts. I had to have the house itself inspected, test the water, look for termites, check the sewage system.

If I wasn't precisely sure how a septic tank worked, I was told by all parties that I wanted the sale to be conditional on there being one and on its being deemed in good working order. Feeling plenty tough, I asked that Georgette write that into the contract.

At her recommendation, I hired a local excavator to determine all of the above.

Joe Bates was the first of the big men in big trucks to drive to my mountaintop that summer, accompanied by his cheerful assistant, Chuckie, an even bigger man with an even larger truck.

These men in trucks grew steadily in number. In July they invaded the mountain in force, returned repeatedly to respond to various crises, and are there still, clearing, sawing, digging, plowing, tinkering. Although, in theory, these were men as unlike me as I could imagine—skilled, competent, mechanical, weathered, rural—we got along famously.

The mountain, I saw, was one big Toys "R" Us for guys, all of whom had the best playthings: customized trucks with four-wheel drive and flashing lights, power tools, chainsaws, guns.

And they were among the world's best bullshitters. No work was more important than the opportunity to talk about it, to recount stories related (or completely unrelated) to it, to razz one another about the inability to do it. The theorizing, philosophizing, lore and mythology that went into digging holes or blasting termites never ceased to amaze me; it was creative, inventive, an ingrained ritual of storytelling.

There was no task, from trapping mice to tearing up dying shrubbery, that didn't present more than one option, drawing a wide range of opinions from associates, friends, and sometimes complete strangers. If the people right around you weren't helpful or knowledgeable enough, D'Aiuto's Bakery, the Agway, and the hardware store attracted a steady stream of men with their trucks idling outside, all happy to dispense wisdom as they made their purchases, bantered with the staff, waited for their change.

These men were innately generous teachers, and they weren't all talk. One let me dowse a well. Another told me how to lay cinder block. I got detailed lectures on raccoons, the ways of deer and bats, the perils of walking dogs in hunting season.

There were wide psychic spaces between us, but the house was the common ground on which we met, neither side quite grasping the other but fascinated nonetheless. I peppered them with questions about gutters and insulation; they wanted to know how books were written and published. I had the sense that despite some mutual suspicions—they thought I'd look down on them, I thought they might look down on me—we were surprised at how much we liked each other.

We did have some things in common. Kids. Dogs. And the peculiar similarities of being, in our separate ways, independent contractors, beset by problems with authority, money worries, and the fickle nature of our customers.

I grew schooled in the ethos of mountain life: everything you see—hills, meadows, forests, boulders—can be moved or rearranged. But don't try to hire people in hunting season. Pay your bills on time—but if you don't have the money with you when you come to buy something, you can drop it off later. Watch all you want, but don't second-guess. Don't offer photo ID when you write checks—it isn't friendly. Believe in four-wheel drive. Complain bitterly about taxes. Be awed by winter. Drive slowly, watch for deer.

Perhaps most important, oppose the growth of government and any form of regulation or bureaucracy. To hear the big men in trucks talk, you'd think federal troops were descending on the valley. As it happened, this township didn't seem overwhelmed by red tape. It had no mayor, police force, fire department, zoning board, municipal building, or school.

As far as I could tell, all the township really offered was a highway department justly famed for effective snowplowing, a planning board and one building inspector, and a grand new dump known as the Recycling and Transfer Station. The only other municipal service I could confirm was that residents were entitled to help themselves to the giant pile of sand, next to the highway building, to promote traction and sure footing in bad weather.

Still, when you mentioned government, the big men all shook their heads grimly and said more or less the same thing: "Things are changing around here, no doubt about it." They talked ominously of paperwork, licenses and fees, new regulations, and newcomers trickling in who want to shut the door behind them.

The big truck Joe Bates had arrived in was blue. Chuckie followed right behind in his own truck. Chuckie sported a beard and cast a huge shadow. His belly made a strong statement beneath his T-shirt. Blessedly, he was a good-humored man. I'd heard that these two were the best excavators in Washington County.

Joe, a tanned and muscular guy with a shock of white hair, was carrying a shovel when I first met him, and Chuckie a massive iron pole six or seven feet long. Both men nodded.

The good news was that this planned search for the septic tank had prompted Lenny's friend to come and remove the jarringly ugly plastic swimming pool, along with the various creatures who'd found it a congenial home. There remained only a wide, sandy swath through the dead grass of the backyard.

Lenny and his friends were incredulous that I didn't want to keep the pool. I'd found a sort of handbook by the fireplace called "The Last Resort Book." On page 29, Lenny had written the pool rules: Add chlorine if the water looks green. No jumping. "Skinny dipping is fine—but no peeing in the pool."

But the book was mum on the subject of sewage.

"Any idea where the tank might be?" asked Joe, staring dubiously at the ground around the house.

I laughed. Joe looked me over, glanced at Chuckie, and smiled. These guys didn't seem to mind if you were ignorant about sewage, so long as you didn't pretend otherwise.

Joe began digging, and Chuckie picked up his iron pole and drove it deep into the ground, first here and then there, again and again. I made small talk, asked silly questions. I couldn't feel at ease watching other people work so hard, but Georgette had instructed me to pay attention.

The sun was fierce on the mountaintop. I brought out soda and ice water. Joe patiently told me about septic tanks and leaching fields and related technologies. Chuckie told dismaying stories about various septic disasters they had encountered. In a few minutes, both men were covered in sweat and dirt. I wondered why there wasn't some digital handheld wand that would beep when it located the tank.

After a few minutes, another pickup pulled into the driveway. This was Bob, a neighbor and former sheriff and friend of Lenny's, there to watch. He had septic stories to tell too, and many others from his days as a former state trooper, when he plowed through five-foot snowdrifts to pull mangled bodies from car wrecks or held angry drunks in headlocks for hours until backup arrived from the next county. "You had to hold 'em," Bob explained. "If you let 'em go, you'd have to shoot 'em."

Yet another pickup truck pulled in carrying two friends of Bob's. Georgette arrived. In short order, there was a circle standing around Joe and Chuckie, speculating as to where the tank was, if there was a tank. Joe had shoveled his tenth or fifteenth hole to no avail, while Chuckie, wielding the heavy iron pole as if it were a toothpick, had poked into the ground at least fifty times.

Meanwhile, the exterminator was crawling through the basement. The architect arrived for the building inspection, looked grimly around, and vanished into the house, clipboard in hand. There were now five, maybe six pickup trucks. A Bell Atlantic truck roared toward the driveway, saw there was no more room to park, and backed out and around to the other side.

Conversations flowed continuously and seamlessly, digging to soil, soil to planting, planting to raccoons, raccoons to "lead poisoning" and then to law enforcement, law enforcement to taxes with a detour to sports, then round again.

"Don't worry about the crowd," Joe assured me at one point. "The difference between us and the people in New York City is that we don't charge for the bullshit."

Joe and Chuckie couldn't find the tank. After some discussion, the decision was to go get the "ho." This gave me some pause, till Bob explained he meant a backhoe.

I had a sinking feeling that the reason they hadn't found the tank was because there wasn't one. There might be a cesspool instead, just a hole in the ground into which sewage flowed. Cesspools were no longer legal. If I didn't have a septic system, we'd need to install one, and who would pay for that?

Joe and Chuckie disappeared, driving off down the mountain. Bob regaled me and several strangers in pickups with additional accounts of his days as a sheriff, facing exiled druggies who grew marijuana in the cornfields, political radicals hiding from the FBI down in Shushan, and sad calls to help women who'd been beaten bloody by their husbands in the dead of winter. He'd seen convicts break out of the county jail up in Salem and hide out in barns for weeks. He'd seen deer crash through windshields on dark country roads.

In a few minutes, the ground shook as Joe and Chuckie backed a huge flatbed truck into my dirt driveway, cracking off branches. Julius and Stanley ran for cover.

My yard soon looked carpet-bombed. It had already been pockmarked with small holes, and now Chuckie, maneuvering the backhoe like it was a tricycle, was making a series of gashes wherever they guessed the tank had to be. Clouds of dust floated off the mountaintop. As Chuckie gouged away strips of turf, Joe poked around with his shovel, so that Chuckie didn't plow through the top of the tank, if there was a tank.

The grass was nearly completely scraped away when I heard shouts of satisfaction. "Got it," said Joe. "Here she is."

I had a septic tank. It was well built, said Joe. It didn't even need pumping.

That was the good news. The bad news, he said, was that it was very close to my well. The well was to the right of the back door, the septic a few paces to the left. They were supposed to be a lot farther apart.

"They probably had no choice but to build it there, because of the shale," said Chuckie charitably, reasoning backward like Sherlock Holmes. "If they had to truck gravel in just to put the house on, then they didn't have many places to go." I had no idea what he meant.

I looked out at the driveway, lined with trucks. I was paying for most of them to be there: the blue construction truck Joe had arrived in, Chuckie's, the giant flatbed for the backhoe. The exterminator was talking to me about the rodent-urine smell he'd picked up in the basement. "Mice." He shrugged. He didn't seem like a man who got excited about mice. The phone man had vanished into the woods.

Joe and Chuckie were packing up. Joe's bill for the morning—three trucks, a backhoe, two workers, four hours—was $250.

MENCKEN WROTE OFTEN about what an inferior species humans are, how hypocritical and arrogant they are to see themselves as superior creatures.

I take his point. Solitude and holiness are often linked to spirituality, but humility may be even more appropriate. I came to the mountain with all sorts of baggage beyond my duffels and my laptop—arrogance and hubris foremost among them. I can now look anybody in the eye and say that I am a far more humble man.

So far on this excursion, I was entitled to feel spiritual only if spirituality was defined as spending money you didn't have. If that were truly the case, spirituality would be available to everybody, at least temporarily.

My hubris lay in buying a place to think and write, in a locale where people earned their calluses by working in very physical ways every day. I knew nothing about living in the country or maintaining a rural household. My cerebral seeking would depend on the labor of the many people I would have to pay to live comfortably on the mountaintop. But only initially. I intended to figure out what I needed to know; I didn't want to be dependent on the kindness or labor of others for too long.

There is an innate attitude of superiority that arises from living in one of the world's most sophisticated urban areas. I saw myself as leaving behind high culture and amenities to settle in a place with neither, a retreat, an escape. All of this sounded—and was—patronizing.

What had never occurred to me was that I was much too inexperienced, at first, to live there safely, wisely, or happily. But after my brush with solitude, my crash course in sewage and water, and various other lessons, I was learning.

The mountain set about teaching me some things. Systematically, almost surgically, it showed me how little I knew, leaving me shaken. I had this disturbing feeling that the mountain had sized me up and decided I was one of those projects best renovated by starting over.

I was humbled on the mountain, in an almost biblical sense, virtually every day. None of these lessons seemed to arrive in predictable ways. Wasn't this part of why I'd come, to get to the core of me? To keep the hinges oiled? To give birth to myself again at fifty?

Yet it was not a process of dramatic revelations or insights; it was vastly more complex and measured. It wasn't a question of running to the mountain, shedding scales, and finding oneself nose to nose with God. It was a matter of heat and bugs and cold, lonely nights, of mastering my house, learning what I could or couldn't control.

Whatever I was seeking—and watching Joe and Chuckie work, I was aware of still not knowing what that was—would only be attained patiently, over time, not with one experience but with hundreds. I would encounter it in the many interactions with my new house, with the mountain, with my family, with nature and seasons, with the people I was meeting, with the new and different culture I was drawn into here, with solitude, with my past.

Spirituality is usually presented in terms of the Big Payoff—Merton finds faith sitting in a church one day. I'd expected something similarly dramatic. It took me weeks to grasp that this was going to be painstaking and meticulous work, hand-to-hand combat of the most intensely personal sort—with myself. Day by day, chore by chore, I'd know more in six months or a year—if I were lucky—than I did now. If I weren't, or felt too shallow and overwhelmed, I'd sell the house, slink off the mountaintop, and die in New Jersey after all.

As it happened, the hinges were not only oiled, they were blown nearly right off the door.

THE ONLY TIME of day I sometimes felt lonely, I found, was dinnertime. Before, I was happy to work in peace. Afterward, I was happy to read, do chores, walk, and brood. But dinnertime on the mountain could be bleak. It was the only time I turned the snowy old TV on, to hear voices while I ate.

I'd make some pasta dish, or maybe a veggie burger, always being sure to prepare vegetables or a salad. Details are everything when you're alone. Full place setting—glass, plate, salad plate, knife, fork, spoon. No eating standing up, no eating on the move, no eating out of the fridge. Ritual was essential in solitude, where time slipped away and the boundaries that defined work and play, sleep and wakefulness, mealtimes and chore times, could blur.

Since he was one of the masters of solitude, I read Merton's copious journals, and my day took on echoes of his. They included contemplation, simplicity, solitude, and plenty of hard work.

I became meticulous, almost fussy about routines, an enormous change for a markedly disorganized person. Get up early, before sunrise. Shower every morning. Make sure to wear clean clothes. Take the dogs for a longish walk, the first of several each day, eat breakfast, settle down to write. Sometimes I drove into Shushan for the paper, which Debbie at Yushak's Market saved for me, sometimes not.

I wrote and made calls, I broke for lunch, then tended to gardening and cleaning tasks. Then more work, a proper dinner, usually while watching the news. Then reading, sitting alone and staring at the mountain, checking in at home. Then a final nighttime walk in woods so dark I had to bring a flashlight to see the path.

Sometimes I felt particularly disconnected, having to redefine the patterns of my days at fifty. A father of a teenaged daughter, I suddenly had hours to fill. A man married for twenty-five years, I woke up and went to sleep alone, long-entrenched rhythms disrupted. The dogs seemed to sag at dinnertime, too, curling up with each other and sighing. For all of us something was missing.

So sometimes I drove down the hill to the Burger Den, a folksy family-run clapboard roadside restaurant with Formica tables and mounted fish and painted saw blades on the walls, to sit at the counter with the other oddballs who, for one reason or another, were eating by themselves. These were mostly big, rough-hewn men, truckers and construction workers, salesmen and cops out on the road. They watched the television hanging over the counter, talked sports and politics, muttered about the weather. They usually checked me out for a minute or two, then gradually included me. I liked talking with them.

"Kids," a farmer—to judge from his sunburnt skin—blurted out one evening, as he sat beside me eating fried mozzarella sticks. "What the fuck are you gonna do?" This elicited groans and mutters of agreement from five seats down.

"Right," I shot back. "What the fuck are you gonna do?" The other men all nodded. I had no idea what the fuck any of us were going to do. Even though I had no real complaints, you couldn't go wrong at the Burger Den counter bitching about kids or the wife.

One night a younger man in a faded Yankees cap turned his bloodshot eyes to me after dessert and quietly announced, "My wife left me today. I could kill her. Or me." Before I could figure out how to respond, he got up and walked out. Another night, a woman whose face was badly bruised borrowed the restaurant cordless to call the sheriff and reported that her husband had struck her again, that she had fled, and could they please go and arrest him, as she had two kids in the house. Nobody talked to or looked at her.

But usually dinners were chatty, more upbeat. The counter was a communal dinner table. If you wanted to be alone, you took a table; sitting at the counter was a sign you wanted company and conversation, though names were rarely exchanged. I was a bit surprised, but pleased, that these men, with their rough hands, let me be one of them.

The waitresses called me "hon" and "doll" and pushed the specials of the day. The health craze hadn't hit the Burger Den. Half the things on the menu were fried, and everything came with globs of butter or dressing or mayonnaise.

Though the place was an invitingly close, two-minute drive down the mountain, I didn't want to become a regular. Like drinking, it was a prop I shouldn't make too much use of. I was working to build new rituals and habits. Fending for myself, learning to be alone, embracing the discipline of solitude—these were things I needed to establish at the outset. Loneliness, even as voluntary as mine, was something I had to accept, not run from. I marveled that Merton survived so much of it, deep in the Kentucky woods.

There was a sadness to some of the men at the counter, a sense of drift. Some were traveling through and needed a meal, but others, like me, just didn't want to be eating dinner without hearing other people's voices. The waitresses, I realized, reminded me of the nurses I'd talked to in the middle of the night in the hospital where Emma had her surgery. They were sympathetic yet businesslike. They were the ones who'd be going home.

LIFE ON THE mountaintop continually surprised me. New Jersey is a moderate place, with few extremes of weather, and plenty of government to respond when they come. Middle-class homes and most public places are air-conditioned in the summer. In the winter, giant plows clear the streets whenever snow accumulates. The lights rarely go out, and if they do, it's seldom more than a few minutes before they're restored.

On the mountain, the weather is more extreme, the official response thinner, and power outages a regular occurrence. Neighbors and bystanders are farther away. You're on your own more; you have to keep your wits about you. It's a challenge.

One day, at a shopkeeper's suggestion, I walked the dogs along the railroad tracks that led from a nearby town into a stand of woods. In New Jersey, every railroad crossing is guarded like the entrance to the White House—gates, bells, red lights. But there were no signs or warnings on this path.

The forest was still and gorgeous, and I was lost in thought, barely noticing that the ground beneath the tracks was dropping away, the wooden ties between the rails growing more sparse.

Before I realized it, we were forty to fifty feet above a rocky river. Julius and Stanley had walked out ahead of me, to the middle of a long trestle, and then, suddenly becoming aware of walking at a considerable height with large gaps between the railroad ties beneath their feet, frozen.

Julius looked balefully at me, tried to move, and slipped, one of his legs dangling below the tracks; Stanley tried to turn back toward me, hobbling precariously along, then stopping. I heard a train sound in the distance, and I had no idea how close it was or whether it was headed our way.

Terrified for all of us, I froze, too, cursing my obliviousness. A fall onto the rocks below would surely have been fatal if the dogs panicked; I couldn't leave them. But sticking around to encounter a train wasn't an attractive option either.

Speaking softly, telling them to stay, I crawled over to Julius, pulled his paw back up onto the wooden slat, then helped him to turn around. There were ample wooden ties and solid ground just fifty feet behind us.

Praying that some agility gene would kick in and give them the confidence to walk without slipping, I led the way. I couldn't bear to turn around and see whether Julius or Stanley slipped or balked. They had come this far out of trust, and I had betrayed that trust by being unprepared for where I was.

I glanced occasionally to see them struggling, walking carefully but moving forward. Stanley actually passed me, then turned around, tail wagging, to greet me. I was trying to keep my own balance, walking rapidly with my arms extended.

"God, Stanley, no," I begged. "Just keep going, keep going." I swear he sensed what I was saying; he turned and walked forward. I heard Julius clacking along behind me and, somewhere behind him, the train's whistle again.

In a couple of minutes, the three of us had reached the end of the trestle, and I was on my knees hugging them. I called them over into the trees; moments later the train chugged slowly past. For days I had nightmares about Julius sliding through the trestle and falling to his death. It was a tough lesson, but I got it.

I got lots of them. There was the afternoon I drove home from an errand through a ferocious thunderstorm, the lightning dazzling and the rain impenetrable. State police and sheriff's cars, fire trucks and pickups with flashing lights were cruising through the town, responding to various crises. The five or six miles to my mountain took nearly half an hour. I had to keep pulling over because the visibility was so poor. It didn't get any better.

Once we reached the house, the dogs and I, already soaked, walked around to the valley side. Black clouds were scudding across the hills. Sheets of rain dimmed the afternoon light. I thought of a Spielberg movie: Dinosaurs should've popped up in the valley below and stalked across to Vermont; the noise wouldn't have been much greater. Most amazing were the mile-high streaks of lightning that broke out of the clouds and flashed vividly to the farms below.

It was a powerful sight, so hypnotic and beautiful that I couldn't stop watching. The dogs, less riveted, took cover by the back door. Poor things; they hated thunder. I stepped back to let them in when a flash filled my eyes, momentarily blinding me and knocking out the power in the house. Not twenty-five feet away, a silver birch split in two.

Watching the spectacle, I walked over to examine the tree; with several limbs wrenched away from the trunk, I wondered if it could survive.

Between booms, absurdly, I heard the faint warble of my phone. I ducked back inside. "Jon," said a voice I could barely hear. "This is Doc, your neighbor. You okay over there? You taking care?"

Interrupted by ground-shaking thunder, I said I'd been outside watching the storm, the most amazing thing I'd ever seen. Was he all right? I asked, wondering why he was calling. Perhaps he wanted to alert me to the beauty of a mountain thunderstorm, something no newcomer should miss.

His reply was drowned out; I asked him to repeat it.

"You're not getting my drift!" he shouted.

What?

"Stay the hell inside," he ordered. "Don't go back outside until it's over. There's a reason that house of yours has a new roof."

THE HUMBLING PROCESS was not always so dramatic, but it was continuous.

It was nearly midnight when I drove back up the highway toward my mountain, after a day in Bennington, Vermont. The outskirts of Bennington were ugly, more like Jersey than Vermont, lined with strip malls and discount houses. I missed my funky neighborhood around the mountain, whose biggest buildings were the Livestock Auction and the Recycling and Transfer Station. The dogs were with me, asleep in the back of the van.

I could see the flashing lights at the bottom of my road from a couple of miles away. A sheriff's car blocked the turn.

"Can't go up there," a young deputy said. "Forest fire. Road's closed."

"How bad is it?" I asked. "I've got a house up there."

He was unmoved. "It's on the other side of the mountain," he said. Not my side, yet. But the summer had been hot and largely dry. I could see smoke rising into a flickering orange sky at the top of the mountain; it didn't seem far from the Last Resort. Deer were bounding down the hillside above me.

I had nowhere to go. Jeff wasn't home. In any event, I didn't dare drive away not knowing if my house was all right. I drove the van across the street, to the shoulder where people parked when they wanted a quick swim in the lake. I let the dogs out—they were trained not to run into the street—and the three of us sat down along the guardrail by the side of the road, like the famous Three Monkeys, to wait.

Far from home, I felt friendless, homeless, foolish.

The dogs and I sat there for two or three hours watching, dozing, yawning, scratching, every now and then one or the other of us getting up to walk along the side of the road and pee on some bush. I wanted to go home to Jersey, hat in hand, acknowledging defeat, but the thought of my Power-Book stopped me. I couldn't leave it up there to burn; my next book was in it. And even though I was still just renting, I felt responsible for Lenny's house.

Around 2:00 A.M., a woman in a Chevy station wagon drove by, stopped, backed up. She took in the dogs and me, leaning against the guardrail.

"You okay?" she asked, lowering her window.

"I guess so. They won't let me up because there's a forest fire." I must have sounded grim.

"You look a little lost," she said.

"You have no idea." I thanked her for her concern.

I could never have told this good woman what I was really thinking: I used to be a big shot, lady. I went to lunch with the people you see on the cover of *TV Guide*. A secretary kept a list of my chores and meetings, made reservations for lunch, cashed checks for me, got me tickets to hot shows, typed and mailed letters. When there were big stories or bad weather, a limo took me to work.

Before I began frequenting the Burger Den, I went to London regularly enough to have a favorite hotel and pub. The maître d's at some of Manhattan's toniest restaurants knew my name, held tables for me, fussed and cooed when I came in.

And why shouldn't they? I managed a megamillion-dollar budget, controlled two hours of national TV airtime every morning. I could interrupt a network program to blast onto the air with "special reports." I dispatched correspondents and producers to breaking stories all over the world, ordered satellites, chartered planes. I was a rising star; CBS executives had their eyes on me.

To be honest, lady, the Big Shot role didn't last long—four, five years, maybe. And it never fit. There was no way that I belonged in that series of jobs or could handle them. I quit one after another, got embroiled in a series of ugly struggles, quite conspicuously failed to produce a successful TV broadcast.

Almost the entire time, I was falling apart, bit by bit, alternately frantic, enraged, terrified. I chain-smoked, drank more than I should have. I was alive to buy a house on a mountaintop only because the Big Shot went down, hard.

The Big Shot returned to his office from lunch one day to find it wasn't there anymore—everything had been moved across the street by some guys in black sweat suits. I languished in exile for a year, slowly unraveling, waiting for somebody—anybody—to return my phone calls. But it was over, of course.

The phone never did ring again. I never got back to London or those fancy restaurants. I never had much money to spend after that, or anything like a sense of security. A significant chunk of income I did have was diverted to purchase necessary but expensive psychiatric help.

When I change my life, lady, I really *change* it. I barely knew anyone from that time anymore, and few people who knew me now had any idea I'd ever been to London, let alone stayed in an eight-room suite with a butler bringing my toast in the morning, or that Diane Sawyer kissed my butt twice a day, more often when she wanted something. Most of the time, I forgot it myself.

Sitting on the roadside as this concerned woman waved, rolled up her window, and drove off, I realized that the Big Shot showed himself only rarely these days.

An hour later, the deputy moved his car and I could drive up the mountain. The fire had been contained on the far side. Everything was safe. For now.

THE NEXT EVENING after dinner I grabbed my walking stick and the dogs and set out into the thick woods behind the house. A quarter mile or so down the road, I knew, was that beautiful meadow with a view west toward the Adirondacks.

Five minutes later, we were lost. I should have reached the meadow by that point, but the trees shut out the sky and it was hard to tell where you were. I had veered off, somehow.

The ground turned swampy. I came across an old stone fence, long fallen apart. The thick underbrush made walking hard.

I stopped to listen for car sounds; the road up the mountain should've been just off to my left, and while it wasn't heavily traveled, there was usually *some* traffic. But I stood for ten minutes and didn't hear a sound. I kept moving to what I thought was my left, but I realized I had no idea what direction I was going in.

I doubted I was really in any danger. This wasn't northern Canada. It was a warm summer evening. There were houses in every direction, no more than a half mile away, even if I couldn't see any.

Eventually, if we kept walking, we'd have to come to the bottom of the mountain, with its state highway. But we'd been walking for more than an hour, and we hadn't come to the highway, or to a house, or to anything at all familiar.

"Home, guys, get us home," I shouted to Julius and Stanley. Both wagged their tails appreciatively, watching me. Lassie could've done it.

We walked for another forty-five minutes or so, dusk approaching, the dogs panting. Mosquitoes began to whine in my ears.

It seemed we might be spending the night out in the woods. I could make a sort of nest from leaves and twigs and just go to sleep. Solitude, round two. I tried piling some leaves into a makeshift pillow, lying down on them. But the leaves dribbled down my shirt, and twigs poked my back. It would be a long night, if it came to that.

I got up and resumed walking.

Here was another stone fence, or perhaps the same one. Stone fences are still often the boundaries around property. Perhaps instead of crossing this one, I should follow it; if it was somebody's boundary, it might lead to a house. In half an hour or so, I'd have to stop, anyway; it was getting hard to see.

The fence, despite some gaps, led to the top of a rise. Following along, partly by feel, I looked down to see a house. And it was lit up. Saved. The dogs bounded ahead, relieved to be spared from their blundering master.

As I plunged down out of the forest, I was stunned to see that the house was my neighbor Doc's—which meant that my own house was just a five-minute stroll down our shared driveway.

My house. The ugly white asbestos shingles looked as appealing as a Newport mansion. It was the first time, I realized, that I'd really thought of it as my house, not Lenny's.

Looking into the woods, I figured that I'd never been more than a hundred yards from it at any time in the several hours I'd been crashing through the underbrush. Getting lost next to my home was a sorry metaphor. Walking in the woods isn't the same as walking on my suburban Jersey street; as with so many things up here, you had to stop and think first.

Back inside, chastened yet again, I found a message from Georgette on my answering machine.

"Jon," her recorded voice announced soberly. "I have some bad news for you. You failed the state water test. Your water is no good."

When I called back, Georgette said she was flabbergasted. This hadn't happened in the five years she'd been selling real estate in Washington County. But the water I'd been drinking had been contaminated with *E. coli* bacteria.

The state tests for two bacteria: coliform and *E. coli*. Coliform comes from mostly natural causes—a well that hasn't been used lets algae build up, or some animal has fallen into the well. *E. coli* is different—it invariably reflects the presence of human waste. Joe Bates had known the second he looked at the septic tank: it was too close to the well.

Heartsick, I felt the little house slipping from my grasp and—feeling foolish about my hike gone wrong—beyond my abilities as well. I knew as much about wells as I did about walking in the woods.

Georgette cautioned me not to drink from the tap. I should get jugs of bottled water for cooking, tooth brushing, dishwashing. Poor Paula, scheduled to pay her first visit to the mountain in two days, would delight in this experience.

"I have to talk to Lenny," Georgette said. "We'll figure out what to do."

THE WELL

But there is a mental ecology too, a living balance of spirits in this corner of woods.

—THOMAS MERTON, *DANCING IN THE WATER OF LIFE*

SO THE FIRST round of big men in trucks was only a prelude to a squadron of much bigger men in much bigger trucks. A few days after the bad news from the state of New York, Clarence Gould led a caravan—his pickup, his son's, two giant drilling rigs—up the mountain, through and sometimes right over the woods, to a spot eight feet from where I sat writing in the rear bedroom of my house. I heard branches snapping and saw small saplings going down.

Clarence was alone in the first truck. He popped out, his hand extended, wearing a faded blue baseball cap, a green shirt and pants, and battered work boots. He was built exactly like a tree trunk, short, solid, his face lined, his skin brown. He exuded competence.

Clarence's arrival followed days of anguished discussions and tortuous negotiations about how to deal with our nasty water.

Paula and I had had a tough weekend trying to figure out what to do. Walk away? Pump chlorine into the well? Install a thousand-dollar ultraviolet purification system? Pay part of the cost of a new well? All of the cost? None of the cost?

Everybody we'd talked to—friends, plumbers, neighbors, contractors, engineers—had an opinion. We didn't want to play hardball with Lenny, a sick man who needed the money. But we didn't want to get stuck with a house that had polluted water.

Of all the advice I'd gotten, what stuck came from a farmer I'd met at the Agway, where I was pouring out my water woes to Alan at the cash register.

The farmer, a large, dust-covered man in a T-shirt and blue baseball cap, was holding a giant bag of lime as if it were a towel slung over his shoulders. He might have been in his sixties or seventies, but his arms were muscled like a twenty-year-old's. His cheek bulged with tobacco, and he listened and looked me over with amusement as I described my miserable well and the various remedies being urged on me.

The farmer—Alan called him Stewart—couldn't take it for more than a few minutes. "Excuse me, son," he interrupted. "Where are you from?"

"New Jersey," I said.

He nodded, as if that explained everything.

That this man and I were having a conversation in upstate New York about my digging a well was nothing short of bizarre, yet no stranger than lots of things that had preceded it.

Stewart volunteered that he had dug a bunch of wells in his time and had watched a bunch of others being dug. He asked Alan for a piece of paper and wrote down his phone number.

"Some people want advice and some people don't," he said. "I can't hang around here now, but if you want to talk, call me at home." I could use some advice, I assured him. In fact, if he would have considered adopting me, I would have jumped into his arms right there and then.

Alan, who spoke of Stewart with considerable respect, seemed impressed that he had even bothered to offer counsel. If anybody in the county knew what he was talking about, Stewart did. So I did call him up, somewhat to my surprise, the second I got home.

Stewart picked up on the third ring. There was a lot of static on the line, and I could hear deafening tumult in the background. He was answering his cell phone, Stewart said, on a tractor out in his back field. He turned the tractor off, quieting the roar, so I could tell him what had happened in more detail.

"The well and the septic are that close?" he said, incredulous. Don't mess with chlorine, he advised. A plumber would dump some down the well, the water would pass the state test and then a month later be polluted again and I wouldn't even know it. Somebody would get sick, and then we'd have a "situation." And don't mess with those ultraviolet bulb gizmos either, Stewart added, especially not if you live in New Jersey and won't be around to know when the bulbs burn out.

"Son, ask them for a new well," he announced. "And don't pay one red cent toward it, either. You don't sell a man a house with bad water. And you don't *buy* a house with bad water. That's all you need to know."

And that was all I needed to hear. I'd told Georgette I wanted a new well or I was gone. It had become the line I wouldn't cross. Within hours, she called back to say Lenny and his family had agreed; they'd pay for the well from the proceeds of the sale. Clarence Gould would arrive in two days. "I hope you're not planning to get much work done this week," she said.

My consultant, Stewart, was still out in his field. He was pleased with my decision and even happier about who was going to dig it.

"Clarence from Pawlet, Vermont?" said Stewart. "He's a good man. He'll get you good water."

I hoped so. I had been filling plastic jugs at Jeff's house for days.

"We don't know what we're doing," Paula reminded me constantly from back in New Jersey. "We're in over our heads." It all made her extremely skittish, and it didn't boost my confidence either. I was growing weary of the house and its assorted problems, tired of the mice, the bugs, the clutter, the debris, the water jugs. This wasn't the creative retreat I'd dreamed about for years; it was a hot, tacky, infested, polluted, claustrophobic mess.

And now that we'd decided to sink a new well, there remained the nail-biting question of whether it would work. If sewage from the septic tank had seeped down through the shale that made up the mountaintop, it might be hard to find good water.

But Stewart told me there was good water all over the mountain. Trust Clarence, he said.

Clarence, I discovered after a couple of trips to the bakery, the hardware store, and the Agway, was a legend. Everybody said he was the best there was, the first one they'd call. His motto, I was told, was "We never leave a man without good water," a creed I was coming to prize. He charged a flat fee—somewhere around three thousand dollars—no matter how long it took him or how deep he had to dig. If he didn't find good water that passed the state test, he didn't get paid. Sometimes it took him two hours to find water, people said, sometimes a week; he might have to dig down only one hundred feet, or he might need to go to eight hundred or deeper. But he hung in there. I was eager to meet Clarence, anxious for his work to get under way, relieved when he came roaring over the hill that morning, his truck leading the procession.

Three of his men began silently putting braces around the wheels and setting up the huge drill. Amidst much screeching, roaring, and clanging, they raised winches and pulled pipe off the flatbeds. When I walked outside to watch, nobody greeted me or even acknowledged my existence.

These men, I could tell, were different from the locals in big trucks, harder and quieter. There was a notable lack of bullshit. Their pace was fast and relentless, almost grim. Clarence's crew was famous around town for working through the winter without gloves, jackets, or hats, in every conceivable kind of weather, always silently. They were real Vermonters, a breed apart.

Clarence did shake my hand.

"You the owner?" he asked.

"The buyer," I said. "I hear you always get water."

"Pretty much."

Unbelievably, he pulled out a wooden dowsing stick. A pilgrim in the Digital Age, I expected he would bring some instrument called a hydrometer and stick it into the ground, whereupon a monitor would flash numbers that told where and how deep to dig.

"You dowse?" I was incredulous.

"Pretty much."

He stopped and looked at me for a bit. "I got a feeling about you," he said. "You want to try it?"

It was one of the high points of my life; I nearly cried.

"Where?" I asked, stammering.

"Wherever it takes you," he said. "I have the feeling you've got the gift. Just stay as far from the septic tank as you can."

"You say this to all the newcomers?" I was suspicious now. "That they have a gift?" But Clarence just studied the ground.

I held the ends in each hand, the V pointing straight out, the way Clarence showed me, and started walking away from the back of the house, toward the driveway.

I felt a pull on the stick, and the point tilted down, sharply and visibly. Definitely a pull. I hadn't moved it at all, yet the feeling went through the stick and into my arms.

"You see that?" I said, excited.

Clarence wasn't excited. "Yeah. Let me try it."

He took the dowsing stick and walked about six feet farther. The stick dipped again.

"Here," he said to his son, who had been watching without a word. "Dig here." Then he shook my hand, got into his truck, and drove off with a small wave. I never saw him again.

"Does that work?" I asked his son.

The younger Gould—in his thirties, I guessed—smiled slightly. "Well, he always dowses, and we always get water," he said. Then after a few seconds' pause, "Course, there's a lot of water up here."

My dogs, who usually stick within inches of me, fell in love with Clarence's crew. They stayed outside all day for the next three days, dozing contentedly in the shadow of the ear-shattering drill, which shook the house with its racket.

The stories about Clarence's workers were true. They arrived as soon as it was light and didn't leave until it got too dark to see. They never broke for lunch that I could see or even went to the bathroom. I later noticed that they ate on the job, reaching into bags for sandwiches and munching as they pulled levers, adjusted the winch, changed the bits. The noise from the drill was so continuous and deafening that the men—none of whom was wearing earplugs—communicated with a private language of hand signals.

As they worked, lavalike streams of pulverized shale poured out of the hole, coursed through my miserably scraped and pocked yard, and ran down the mountain. The ooze had an odd, earthy, burning smell.

I tried to keep working even as the house shook so badly that the window shade fell off.

Periodically I came out and shouted, "Does anybody want anything to eat or drink?" The men just shrugged. I took this to be a yes and drove down to the Burger Den for a box of hamburgers and Cokes. The men never said anything as I set the box on the hood of one of the trucks and went inside. But at night the sodas and burgers were gone.

The second morning, I drove to D'Aiuto's Bakery and ordered six black coffees.

"That's a lot of coffee," the woman behind the counter observed.

"Yeah, I have guys digging a well."

"Oh, you must be that writer up near Doc's," she said, making sure the caps sat right on the cups.

By the end of Day Two, I was getting alarmed. I asked Clarence's son how deep the crew had drilled.

"Five hundred feet," he said.

"Is that deep?" I asked.

"You bet."

"Do you always find water?" I asked.

"Pretty much."

The mound of shale was approaching a small mountain in itself. I was nearly deaf from the din. It rained the second afternoon, and the men were so covered in grayish mud that I couldn't tell them apart. Julius and Stanley stayed right with them, also covered in grime. At night I had to hose them down.

There were only two sections of pipe left on the third morning. I had the sinking feeling I was going to be one of Clarence's rare failures. Poor Lenny. He'd never sell the house if they couldn't find water.

"We're down to six hundred feet," Clarence's son told me.

"You worried?" I asked.

Not noticeably. "Tomorrow, we're bringing up the Hydro-Fractor truck."

It sounded like something out of Tom Swift. Clarence's son explained that sometimes, when a well got deep, dust and debris from the digging blocked the shaft and kept water from flowing. When that happened, they called in the Hydro-Fractor. A truck was available the next morning.

The way it worked was, a pipe and hose attached the mouth of the well to the truck, which blasted a stream of water down the hole at enormous force. It dislodged dirt and debris and sent water streaming out into the fissures and cracks. Then the water flowed back to the hole, pulling additional water from the surrounding rock. I decided to take his word for it.

The next morning, a venerable green truck with HYDRO-FRACTOR hand-stenciled on its side joined the other trucks. Word had spread that this extreme measure was being taken, which drew spectators and still other trucks. Soon two or three men, arms folded, were leaning against their pickups, watching intently to see if Clarence and the gang had scored again. Georgette was on hand too, along with my neighbor Bob. Doc stopped by. A Jehovah's Witness appeared out of nowhere to hand around some religious pamphlets.

This isn't a house, I thought, it's a movie set—and the movie is about a rumpled, overweight, middle-class man who buys a mountain house thinking it will be a simple place to write. He is eaten alive by bugs, struck by lightning and forest fires, lost in the woods, sickened by infected water, assaulted by waves of mice, divorced by his wife, and bankrupted.

Every one of these men, every truck, every hole gouged in the ground was a message—in fact, the same message: Katz, you're not a pilgrim in search of spirituality, you're a garden-variety boob, overreaching and getting one of the lessons of your life. You deserve whatever you get: plagues, misery, discomfort, and ruin.

Muttering to myself in this vein, I picked up a dozen Cokes at the Burger Den, and some muffins. By now, the waitress at the Burger Den's take-out window and I were becoming friends. "You running a camp up there?" she asked.

Passing out the goodies, I was too nervous to watch what was going on. If this didn't work, it was clear there'd be no house on the mountain. I planned to pack up my stuff and leave that afternoon. If it did work, I had agreed to buy a place I already suspected might be cursed.

I went inside, into my makeshift study, scraping against wicker baskets of dried flowers, muddying up the yellow shag carpeting. I turned my computer on and tried to log on to the Internet. I needed some E-mail from the outside world. The party-line operator came on. I pulled the shades down, put my hands over my ears, waited.

I heard a machine crank up, then some shouts, then a thunderlike boom that shook the mountaintop. I ran outside, but nobody was ready to offer any opinions. "Have to wait a bit," said Clarence's taciturn son, though he was by far the chattiest member of the crew. Meanwhile he and the others began loading up the wires, winches, wrenches, and chains. One way or the other, they would soon be gone.

Another truck pulled down the far end of the driveway. The Return of Joe Bates and Chuckie. They were going to dig a trench and run a pipe from the new well to the basement. The trench would rip up any stretch of the yard not already torn up by the search for the septic tank.

"What if they don't find water?" I asked Joe.

He laughed. "Clarence always finds water," he said.

It was too much for me. As Chuckie rolled the backhoe off the truck and began digging down deep enough to keep the pipe from freezing in subzero winters—at least four feet deep, young Gould had suggested—I piled the dogs into my van and headed for town.

I picked up some groceries, let Jeff's cat out, and then had lunch at the Burger Den, where I sat at a table by myself, eating a BLT on toast and homemade apple crisp. My waitress friend came over. I told her the story of the house and the well, including my confusion about which way I wanted things to go.

"Oh, you've got water, believe me. You know how I know?"

I shook my head.

" 'Cause you say you can't afford the place. That means you'll get it for sure."

I wasn't sure whether to pray that Clarence had found water or that he hadn't. But now it had been nearly three hours since the Hydro-Fractor's blast. A familiar rumbling made me glance up at a darkening sky. Jeez, another storm. I headed back.

Coming up the mountain, I saw the Hydro-Fractor truck racing down the hill. At the house a giant trench, five feet wide and four feet deep, slashed across the yard. The pipe had already been laid, to my shock, and Chuckie was rushing to refill the trench with dirt, already turning to mud as the showers began. The lightning flickering across the valley was considerably less beautiful to me this time, especially when I saw the light in my office go out.

As the rain grew heavier, Clarence's crew got positively animated, scrambling to pack up the trucks and get moving. "Your power's out, so we can't get the well going. We got to get out of here," yelled Clarence's son over the din. "These trucks get hit all the time. We're right on top of the mountain."

"Hey," I shouted at Clarence's son, whose name I didn't know. "Do I have water?"

"I think so," he said. "We got some water into the well. But we can't turn the pump on, so we haven't run it through the pipe, so we can't be sure. Let me show you how to turn it on, 'cause we'll be gone."

Chuckie was scraping the last mounds of dirt over the trench. They'd be back in the morning to tidy up, Joe yelled, and he and Chuckie backed the hoe up onto his flatbed and took off.

I went into the basement with Clarence's son.

"You got to throw this switch when the power comes back on," he began, pointing to a lever on top of a tank. "Then you got to turn this faucet." He indicated a faucet on the ceiling. "Then you got to wait till this gauge hits sixty, down here. Then you got to hit this lever. But wait till the power comes on."

Outside, the familiar booming was making it hard to hear. I wanted to shout to Clarence Junior and the crew to wait, not to abandon me. "You sure you want to leave this to me?" I asked him pleadingly, already forgetting what to switch and what to turn and in what order.

"We got to leave," he said, shaking my hand. "I poured some chlorine in to clean out the pipes. Don't drink the water till the chlorine smell is gone. Leave the faucets running a couple of hours a day, then wait a few days and you can test the water."

The loaded trucks began to pull away. Suddenly, the second truck stopped and one of the workers, a lean man who'd never uttered one word in the four days he'd been here, jumped down from the cab and came over.

He patted Julius and Stanley. "Nice dogs," he said, then he sprinted back to the truck, which drove off.

I was alone on the mountain, in the middle of another storm, surrounded by piles of shale and mud, without water or power. I went onto my tiny front porch with Julius and Stanley, both of whom were soaked, mud-coated, and bedraggled. I'd grabbed the Glenlivet from the kitchen cabinet, and I took a long pull. "We're quite a picture, guys," I said.

The mountain across the way put on another sound-and-light show. This storm was less intense than the first, but it was still an hour and a half before the lights came on. Meanwhile, Doc thoughtfully called to make sure I wasn't dancing around on the mountaintop again like Julie Andrews in *The Sound of Music*.

I still wasn't sure whether I had water or not, whether it was any good, whether this would be my house. Or whether I could remember how to turn the water on.

But with the power restored, I walked around to the back of the house, sinking into the mud that was now my backyard. The storm had cooled the mountain off, and a crisp breeze was blowing back the flies and the clouds. Sunbeams streaked across the valley.

I took a deep breath.

I carried a flashlight, a hammer, and a screwdriver, ready for anything. Pulling open the basement doors, I noticed a dead mouse in the corner, one not even killed by my traps. Maybe the sight of Katz the Mouse Slayer simply scared him to death.

I pulled the string on the basement lightbulb and took a deep breath. I recalled little that Clarence's son had told me. But I gave myself a pep talk. I could figure this out. This was stuff I had to know. Time to show we can grow and learn, even at fifty.

I figured out which lever turned on the water pump and pulled it. Silence at first, and then the joyous sound of water streaming through the pipe on the ceiling, the one that led outside to the trench and then to the well. I yelled for joy, banging my head on the low ceiling. Feeling a tad Natty Bumppo-ish myself, I picked up the dead mouse by the tail, stepped to the top of the basement stairs, and slung him neatly into the woods.

But I wasn't done. Back in the basement, I managed to turn the proper faucet—okay, the only faucet—and saw the gauge on the water tank rising to 60. I pulled the other lever.

Could I have done this? Could I have turned on my new well, hooked it up to the house, and gotten water flowing myself?

I ran outside, around to the side door and into my kitchen, the dogs hot on my heels. I turned on the kitchen-sink faucet, poured the water into a glass, took a gulp, and gagged on the chlorine. Too soon.

But still, water! A strong, clear, cool burst, even if it did reek of chlorine. And I did it! Well, a tiny part of it.

I called Jeff and left a message on his machine. I called Paula and left a message on hers. I called Joe Bates. I called Georgette, my mother, my agent. In an hour, the whole county would know, and when I went into the bakery the next morning, I'd probably get congratulations along with my coffee.

Outside, I did a bit of a jig in the mud. Julius and Stanley danced with me, the two of them barking and jumping around as I whooped and yelled.

I was soaked; my shirt was clinging to my skin, my sandals squishing. I sank to my ankles and raised my fists to the sky in triumph.

LAST RESORT

The way of faith is necessarily obscure.
We drive by night.

—THOMAS MERTON, *THE ASCENT TO TRUTH*

WITH THE WELL functioning and my tap water testing bacteria-free, all that stood between me and ownership of the house was a few days. The closing was scheduled for early August in Saratoga Springs, just before my birthday. Lenny, too sick to attend, had assigned power of attorney to a local lawyer. He was in a Long Island hospital, I was told, but had managed a bedside party for his friends.

Paula sent me her power of attorney as well, along with an envelope full of certified checks. This was a rare delegation of fiduciary authority—the odds of my hanging on to piles of paperwork and getting it all to a lawyer's office in coherent order were slim. Paula was traveling on a story that week, but I also believed she just couldn't bear to participate.

I had always ducked this kind of responsibility, advancing the dubious conceit that the details of ordinary life and finance were beyond me. Which was definitely one of the reasons why I owed money. The role I had adopted was the Fool, too incompetent, addled, or distracted to be entrusted tasks like balancing the checkbook.

For Paula this was sometimes frustrating, since it created more work for her, but it also allowed her to indulge her control-freak tendencies. She paid the bills, gave Emma her allowance, calculated the taxes, dealt with plumbers, insurance agents, and accountants. I got to avoid the banal details of life. If it wasn't the healthiest understanding, it was symbiotic, working for each of us in different ways.

But one consequence of my having run to the mountain was that sometime in July, despite his decades of faithful service, I decided to can the Fool. It was a heartless act, typical of times in which security, compassion, and loyalty barely exist. We had become embroiled in something of a power struggle, and it was either him or me.

In my previous life, I had fired or laid off scores of people. I had done it calmly and surgically, though not without remorse, because there were always plenty of good rationales. A paper was dying and needed to be leaner. Television was changing and budgets were shrinking. I once was told to lay off thirty people in a single day, and I did.

In my decade as a writer, I rarely thought of those ruthless times any longer, except to wince or cringe when I remembered the people and the painful scenes we had shared. But, as with riding a bike, once you've learned how, you never really lose the touch. The Fool didn't fit into my vision of life on the mountain.

The Fool had been especially active on my mountain journey. He stood out on the mountain in a dangerous lightning storm; he got lost in the woods; he walked out onto a railroad trestle with his dogs and then nearly fainted in terror.

Like a dog who shows his belly to a foe, the Fool made the locals laugh and feel comfortable. The Fool was also the toast of many nonrural lunches and dinner parties, with his colorful tales of life upstate.

All these stories and experiences were true but only part of the truth. What I didn't tell people was that it was hard up here, challenging, frightening, disorienting, lonely. I was being not only foolish but also dramatically more resourceful and conscientious. I was taking more responsibility for myself, learning what I didn't know. I astonished myself, after the first few weeks, not with what I couldn't do but with what I could.

This was like ending a long and complicated marriage. The Fool and I had been through a lot together. Still, indispensable at times, he'd become an obstacle.

I fired him on a hot July day. "You're toast, Fool," I announced. "No severance, no counseling. You will undoubtedly have no shortage of offers. Go take one; you're outta here."

The Fool was shocked, speechless. Then he recovered, and complained bitterly. I was ungrateful, he said. He had done a great job for me, he argued, making everybody feel better about me, making me feel safer. He'd been at my side for decades, he pointed out, ever since I'd figured out that telling stories would sometimes interrupt the screaming in my household and make my sister laugh. I'd regret it, he said.

The Fool huffed and took off down the mountain. As he skulked away, I felt relief, followed by a rush of anxiety. Now there was nobody to take care of me but me.

I stashed all the papers, forms, and checks for the closing in a blue cardboard folder and kept it nearby at all times.

THE MORNING BEFORE closing day I had tea with Doc, my good-natured neighbor, a gracious host and ready philosopher, especially about death, which he had seen much of in his medical practice.

Doc used to live in the village, but when he retired he had moved to this quiet, inaccessible part of the mountain. There he had perfected the sort of daily rituals I was learning to develop: the first cigar lighting in the morning, a regular nap in the afternoon. Every morning at precisely the same time, he drove down the driveway—slowly, once he saw I had dogs—to get his mail.

A slightly formal man, he projected warmth and dignity. I had the sense that doctoring had been a sometimes painful calling, and that he thought about it often. He especially remembered "the ones that got away"—the patients he couldn't treat, help, or convince to help themselves. In my New Jersey town, parents rush their kids to pediatricians whenever they cough; here, for many people, medical care was occasional, sometimes forgone.

Doc talked about the losing fights with alcoholics, heart patients, and chronically ill children. Then about acceptance—realizing the limits of what a doctor can say, do, or persuade others to do. And about death. Doc was heading for seventy. The idea stops being remote, he said softly.

"Most people put off dealing with death until the last minute," he said. "But doctors in my position see it differently. They learn to live with it."

Through his stories—the characters never had names—I got some feeling for the harder, less folksy side of life around the mountain: the depression, the drinking, the drugs, the smoking, the poor diets, the grinding poverty and scarce opportunities.

Snipping the end of his cigar, he took a puff and recalled Lenny's last visit to the mountain, just a couple of weeks before I'd first arrived. Lenny hadn't looked well; the whites of his eyes had been bright yellow. Lenny had joked about his eyes, said Doc. But it wasn't hard for my neighbor to recognize a man in decline. He'd seen it often enough.

"He was a good man," Doc said. "A nice man. He was very fond of that house."

He took another puff, and one topic led to another.

He'd been an avid follower of Merton's writings and was eager to talk about them. But we ended up back with Lenny and life. Ever the physician, Doc was still working out Lenny's failing health. "Lenny lived the way he wanted to live." Though Lenny was only in his forties, the conversation had the air of a eulogy.

LATER THAT MORNING came word, via Georgette, that Lenny had been moved from the hospital to a relative's house.

If he died, the house would become part of his estate, my lawyer told me, and would go into probate. It could be months before I would be able to buy it. Georgette had assured me that even if he died, Lenny's family would still want to sell me the house.

But I think only Georgette really understood that if Lenny died before the closing, there was little chance I would wind up buying the house. I wouldn't want to wait months, unable to fix the place up because it didn't belong to me yet. And I doubted that even I could withstand common sense and logic for that long.

It's easy, even exciting, to be impulsive for a few weeks. But over months the fact that I couldn't afford this house, that my wife didn't really want it, that my daughter had never seen it, would sink in.

Up here by myself, clacking away at my keyboard, staring at the mountains, driving to the farm stand down the road for fresh fruit and vegetables, taking the dogs and a book to my secret spot on the Battenkill, I could cling tenaciously to my conviction that I had come here for a good reason.

Back home in the car pool, I wouldn't be so sure.

So on closing day I was anxious, expectant. I got up at 5:00 A.M. and sat outside with the dogs awhile, reading from Merton and H. L. Mencken. Merton was an antidote to Mencken's cynicism, Mencken a check on Merton's joyous spirituality. If I could find a position somewhere in the middle . . .

At eight my lawyer's secretary called.

"Bad news," she said. "We just discovered you don't have a legal right-of-way. You are technically landlocked, without guaranteed access to the road on the mountain. It looks like we will have to postpone the closing."

The long dirt driveway I shared with Doc ran from his house past my driveway and out to the road. It had never crossed my mind that I didn't own it or have the legal right to drive over it. Neither did Doc, actually. From my house to the road was the property of people who owned the white house down the slope, whom I hadn't met or even seen.

Landlocked. It seemed more like a term out of a Patrick O'Brian novel about the Royal Navy than a condition on a small parcel of land in upstate New York. It would be hard to imagine a more worthless piece of property, with the possible exception of a landlocked house with bad water.

My lawyer, who came on the phone, explained that rights-of-way were complex in rural areas. Many had been granted informally, by verbal understandings, generations ago. Neighbors trusted one another's handshakes and rarely bothered to formalize or record them. Courts generally recognized rights-of-way that had been in use for long periods without challenge. But the bank wasn't willing to take a chance. Either we found some record of a legal right-of-way, or the closing would be off.

Lenny's attorney was already on the way up the mountain, my lawyer reported, visiting neighbors in the hope someone might have some written record in a lease or deed.

What a strange snag, after coming this far. This house had fought me every single step of the way, I reflected bitterly. It was a good and practical house, well built and beautifully located, and I wanted to live in it, but something about it didn't want to be sold. I think it was Lenny.

I didn't like the way this closing was shaping up anyway, a race against time while the seller hovered near death. What if Lenny was hanging on just to see the house sold? What if someone had him on some sort of life support until we got through the closing?

When I called Georgette to tell her about the right-of-way, there was a long pause on the end of the line. "Lord," she said. "This started out to be such an easy deal. Now, I've never had a sale get so complicated and dramatic." She stopped to think for a minute.

"The closing can't be delayed," she said quietly. I had no trouble interpreting that: Lenny wouldn't live that long.

"And you won't stick around to rent for months, will you?"

I hesitated. But Georgette had been scrupulously honest; the least I could do was return the favor.

"I won't kid you," I said. "I don't think I'll stick it out. If this falls through, I'll just head home, maybe look for another place someday."

"Go to Saratoga," she said. "We will have to find a way."

I left the dogs sunning themselves on Jeff's lawn with Lulu and headed west on Route 29, through Greenwich and Schuylerville, past the Revolutionary War battlefield, past farms and produce stands.

En route, I called Georgette on my cell phone. She'd been trying to reach me. Lenny's lawyer and Doc had found an old deed that recorded the right-of-way for both our houses. The closing was on.

THE LAWYER'S OFFICE was in a nondescript bank building surrounded by the brick-and-frame Victorian shops and homes of the old spa town. I stopped at a Starbucks nearby for provisions.

Georgette was waiting for me near the receptionist's desk, looking pleased.

Her commission on the sale of this little house, given the dozens of hours she'd patiently put in, saving the deal a dozen times, probably amounted to less than the minimum hourly wage. I was grateful. We hugged each other in the lobby.

My lawyer had a foot-high stack of documents for me to sign and said it would take an hour or so to explain it all.

"Look," I said. "Let me be honest. If my wife were here, she'd pore over every one of these. But I'm really not interested in wading through all that paperwork. I trust that you've protected my interests, and I'm not legally savvy enough to spot it if you haven't. I'm delighted to be getting the place, and I brought coffee and muffins, so let's skip the formality. Just tell me where to sign."

The lawyer hesitated and looked at Lenny's lawyer, who shrugged and glanced at Georgette.

"Great," she said. "Usually I leave when I get the real-estate agent's check, but I think I'll stick around. This could be fun."

As it happened, the closing *was* fun. The lawyers and I signed papers at warp speed, mine making perfunctory efforts at explaining one nuance or another. Lenny's got up every few minutes to make an unexplained phone call, then returned. Mostly, we started bullshitting. Upstate, not even lawyers seemed immune.

I talked about writing mysteries, and we traded possible plots. The lawyers talked about their upcoming vacations in Maine and Martha's Vineyard. We considered how ironic it was that for some people upstate was a vacation, for others a place they needed a vacation from. Georgette told stories of weird houses she had sold and the even weirder people who bought and sold them.

Over coffee and muffins, we joked and chatted and slung the paperwork. We were all sorry when a secretary came in and said the parties for the next closing were waiting outside.

I had a sudden, disturbing thought of Lenny. "I know this sounds strange," I blurted, "but I'd hate to think that Lenny was on life support or something, being kept alive till this closing was over. I'd feel as if I were contributing to his death in some way."

The lawyers looked at each other. "Lenny isn't conscious," said one. "You have nothing to do with his life or death."

So we traded phone numbers and cards and slapped one another on the back.

"Congratulations," my lawyer said, offering his hand.

The house was mine.

I felt proud and happy, imagining my long, sweet, creative summers and family weekends in the country. I didn't want to add to our financial burdens or Paula's stress, but I'd worked out the particulars in my mind, carefully and often. In the fall, I expected to sign a new two-book contract for my mystery series—the sixth and seventh titles. I might even get a bit of a raise, and royalties were bound to start flowing sooner or later.

Meanwhile, I was hatching a proposal for a novel. Plus, there was the nonfiction book, loosely inspired by Thomas Merton, that I'd finish in the fall.

Not only was I avoiding fiscal irresponsibility, I was being downright farsighted. For the first time since leaving TV, I wouldn't be constantly worried about money. We'd have more than enough to start fixing up our dilapidated New Jersey house as well as this new one. Gone would be the garish carpeting and the dark paneling, the fake-wood ceiling beams, the tiny sunbaked porch.

MY FIRST OFFICIAL act after picking up the dogs was to rush into the house and begin pulling wreaths and wicker, drinking slogans and other gewgaws off the walls. Lenny's wife was sending a truck later in the week for the few pieces of furniture and artwork she wanted, but much of the clutter had just become dispensable.

For a month I'd been surrounded by someone else's very personal taste. Now I wanted to lay claim to this place, put my mark on my house.

For an hour I was nearly possessed, stuffing cartons and bags with trash, piling plastic tables and curtain rods into the van. Then I headed to the town dump four miles down the road.

In New Jersey, trash, like water, is a daily reality of life but not my problem. We stuff it into big green bags and put it in plastic cans. Once a week the town sanitation department— our own version of big trucks—cruises by, pulls the bags out of the cans, takes the stuff away. Recycling day for plastic, glass, cans, and newspapers is Wednesday, in my neighborhood, and once a month, on bulky-trash pickup day, we can leave furniture or old appliances on the curb.

We rarely meet the men who perform all these tasks, and if they stood around trading stories, that would constitute scandalous slacking at taxpayers' expense. One or more grumpy citizens would fire off a letter to the local paper.

Whereas the Washington County Recycling and Transfer Station is one of the focal points of life on and around the mountain, a crossroads of technology, environmentalism, and traditional rural life.

On Saturdays, the busiest of the four days it's open, you see everyone you know there.

It's a long white shed open on one side, lined with bins and signs. Household garbage, required to display a one-dollar county trash sticker on each plastic bag, goes into a huge cement pit at one end. There's a bin for cardboard, one for plastic containers, one for colored glass, for clear glass, for wood. More bins for cloth, scrap paper, plastic bottle caps, metal bottle caps.

You pull up with a loaded trunk or backseat and, under the close scrutiny of the staff, distribute each item to the appropriate barrel, bin, or box. On the way, you naturally encounter your neighbors and fellow taxpayers, many of whom pause to bullshit about the weather, the trash, or the Recycling and Transfer Station itself.

Three or four county workers in blue shirts and pants are on hand to assist. They even rush over to cars driven by women and old people to take their bags for them. Although the workers are courteous and responsive, they don't tolerate even the slightest deviation from the rules. And they want you to keep moving; bullshitters pull their Jeeps and pickups over to the right and stand around in chatty clusters, out of the way.

I was carrying a full load of Lenny's stuff I couldn't wait to get rid of. I'd unscrewed the curtain-rod holders and pulled off the pink-and-white lace swags that framed each window. I had a near-complete set of highball glasses. I wondered into which bin to toss trivets and mantelpiece sculptures.

One of the county men noticed the curtains immediately. He gestured toward a small red Honda across from the loading bins. "Betty is here," he said quietly. "Why don't you just leave these by the wall here?" I didn't quite get what he meant, but I laid the curtains and the rods on the asphalt, deposited my bags of trash and recyclables, then pulled over to the bullshit pen on the right. Half a dozen trucks were idling there, several with dogs peering out of the cab windows. Their owners were busily kicking around crop prices, sports, the weather. I dawdled around the bins, waiting to see what happened.

Betty turned out to be a small, elderly woman in a battered old hatchback. After a few minutes, she struggled out of her tiny car, walked slowly and painfully across the drive holding a piece of cardboard, tossed it into the cardboard bin. She was wearing a washed-out housedress and sneakers with holes in their toes.

She seemed startled to see my castoffs, exclaiming, "Oh, my, curtains! Why, I could give these to my daughter Jenny. She just might like them." The recycling worker, happening by, agreed. "Sure, take them, Betty. They'd be good for your kid."

Strolling closer to her car, I noticed when she opened her hatch that it was stuffed with treasures: lampshades, some linens, a stack of dented plastic bowls. In fact, there were four or five old cars in a row behind Betty's, all driven by women of varying ages, a few with small children, who also seemed to be eagerly scanning the drop-offs. One after another—they apparently took turns—they walked across the lot to toss something into the trash, then "discovered" a window shade, a not-very-broken table, or some other object that somebody like me was tossing out.

They wouldn't accept anything offered directly, the worker explained sotto voce, when I asked about this informal system. So the thing to do was to leave anything salvageable along the wall. "If it doesn't move, somebody will come and take it," he said. "There's some real poor people in the hills around here, and at the end of the day, there's usually nothing left against this wall."

WHEN I DROVE back from the dump, I noticed an enormous truck parked along the roadway near my drive. I wondered if somebody had broken down or gotten lost.

I grew more concerned when I pulled into my driveway, let the dogs out, and saw the fur on their backs bristle, as it did when they'd seen a dog they didn't like or sensed some other danger. Then I saw a shadow passing in front of a living room window shade, and my heart started thumping. Whoever had parked on the roadside must be inside.

There was no 911 to call here, and even if I called the state police, the intruder would have plenty of time to hack me to bits, have a snack, throw a ball for the dogs, and drive off at leisure before help could arrive.

The smartest course would have been to rush down the mountain to rouse Bob, the ex-sheriff and former state trooper. But my cover was already blown, since the dogs had charged to the door and were barking furiously. I couldn't leave them, and I didn't really have time to slink away.

Anyway, what thief or worse would strike in broad daylight, leaving his highly identifiable rig on the road for every passerby to spot?

I opened the door; if there was trouble, we'd get on with it. The dogs charged through the kitchen and into the living room, where I heard joyous exclamations, the silly cooing of a dog nut.

"Lenny?" came a voice from inside. "Where's the shar-peis?"

The tall, swarthy, big-bellied man in the living room was as amazed to see me as I was to see him. "Who are you?" he asked, not unpleasantly. He was holding a glass of my Glenlivet.

"I live here," I replied. "Who are you?"

"Where's Lenny?" he said. "I'm a friend of his. I come up every summer. He gave me a key, but the door was open anyway."

He looked around the room at the watercolors of Cape Cod I'd hung. "I thought his taste in art changed. And," he said approvingly, holding up the Scotch, "his taste in booze has definitely improved."

The guy was a trucker, one of a number that Lenny invited to come up and use his house each summer. Something of an annual event, he told me. A good time was always had. More guys would probably be coming by. I might think of changing the locks, he advised. Not that anybody would steal anything, this was a nice crowd. But there was the question of privacy.

I told him the sad news about Lenny's deteriorating health. He was taken aback. "I've been on the road. I hadn't heard. I'm not that surprised, though," he said. "He looked bad last year."

He shared one more drink with me, and I walked him back down the driveway to his truck. He waved good-bye as he rumbled away. I almost invited him to come back next summer but stifled the impulse. Instead, I went inside and called a locksmith.

I WAS DEFINITELY in the mood for a monklike meal. I'd stopped at the local food co-op for a fresh loaf of seeded wheat, at my farm stand for tomatoes, peaches, and some fresh mozzarella. If there was a breeze to keep the flies at bay, I planned to sit out back with my supper and the dogs and savor becoming a mountaintop property owner.

But the phone rang before I could make the sandwich.

It was Lenny's wife. "Mr. Katz?" she asked, her voice breaking. "I thought I should let you know that Lenny passed away this afternoon. I'll send a truck up in a few days to get his things and anything you don't want."

I offered my sympathy. Beyond that, I had no idea what to say. I'd never met Lenny or his wife, yet here I was sitting in the kitchen he'd built, getting word that he'd died. "I'll take good care of the place," I mumbled.

I learned later that his lawyer's calls during the closing had been to ensure that Lenny was alive until the papers were signed.

It was precisely what I hadn't wanted to happen, his death in juxtaposition to my acquiring the house. Joy no longer seemed appropriate, and neither was my frantic remodeling.

Lenny built the house I was trying to denude of decor. If his death wasn't noted, he had every right to come back and haunt me.

It seemed right—necessary—to invent some farewell ritual here at the mountaintop house he'd built with his father, visited so often and happily, opened up to his friends and fellow truckers. There was nobody else to do it.

I rolled the Formica bar from the shed where I'd stashed it, onto the lawn, next to where the pool had stood. I covered the bar with a spare sheet. In the kitchen, I found a hideous purple candle with silver glitter mixed into the wax and brought it out to the plastic altar. Then I placed "The Last Resort" book on the table by the candle.

"The Last Resort" was a red-covered spiral notebook from Rite Aid; the Post-It on its cover read, "Don't Let Anything Touch the *Radiators!*"

This book had transfixed me since I found it near the fireplace. It was the story of the house, a look inside its innermost workings, a window onto its former owner's soul. I considered Lenny a fellow author.

There were chapters about the TV and VCR, a list of elaborate electrical idiosyncrasies, directions for driving to Vermont. There were instructions for winter, involving turning off the water pump. A list of friends' numbers in case of emergencies. The aforementioned pool rules. And a section—with exclamation points—entitled "Thunderstorm!" I should have read it much earlier.

The fireplace rules were especially elaborate, with information on how to lift up a plate in the grate and sweep ashes into an invisible chute; there was even a sketch of how to lay a fire, with arrows identifying the balled-up newspaper, the kindling, the logs.

To complete the altar, I added a glass with what remained of my Scotch, along with Lenny's WE RUN A TIGHT SHIP, BUT SOME OF US HAVE BEEN GETTING TIGHT A BIT TOO OFTEN sign. Leafing through a volume of Merton's journals called *A Search for Solitude*, a book I was coming to know by heart, I located the passage I wanted. We needed a priest up here, and we had one; Merton was going to make himself useful.

First, I read aloud from my favorite passage in "The Last Resort," on the subject of divining the weather. You could turn on WSPN in Saratoga, advised Lenny, or 102.7 in Manchester. You could read the paper or check the TV. But, he said, "the best local way for you to see the weather forecast is by looking out the kitchen window."

A respectful pause.

"Good-bye, Lenny," I said. "Sorry we didn't meet. I'll take good care of your house."

Then, by flashlight in the gathering darkness, I read from a prayer Merton had said for a dead friend:

> *I have cried to thee and Thou O God has heard me:*
> *O incline Thine ear unto me and hear my words:*
> *Keep me, O Lord, as the apple of Thine eye.*
> *Protect me under the shadow of Thy wings.*
> *Hear, O Lord, my justice—attend to my supplication.*

Then I blew the candle out.

. . .

AFTERWARD, I DISMANTLED the altar and sat for a while on the porch, watching the moon break out of the clouds and then disappear again.

The symbolism was almost too much: closing day, one man leaving life, the other moving into his house. Two spirits on the mountaintop, brushing against each other.

Lenny had died too soon, leaving a young son, an about-to-be-ex-wife, a loving family, and this house that was dear to him. He had many more friends than I, and a gift for having good times with them. In some ways, that made him a richer man.

But what I had, I would probably get to cherish longer. I expected to see my daughter grow up, and to step into old age hand in hand with my wife. And, of course, I had this house.

Lenny, who'd struggled to keep his house for as long as he could, had given me a gift in return for the patched-together, oddball memorial service I'd presided over. He'd made me feel, for the first time, good about what I had done. From our talks, his book, and the house itself, I had some sense of his spirit. I could picture him instantly understanding why I'd wanted this place, even when so many others were rolling their eyes.

"Of course you ought to buy it," he'd surely say. "It's a great place to hang out, drink, light a fire, watch the snow. What the hell."

His death was a reminder that since life is, in fact, short, it is sometimes worth taking risks, plunging in directions that aren't necessarily sensible. Wasn't that how to keep the hinges oiled?

And mine needed oiling. My friendships meant the world to me. Could I keep them, perhaps have more? Be more open to people's invitations and approaches?

Could I do more than stare at nature appreciatively? Learn some of what had to be fascinating details about what I was gazing at?

Could I, a father about to send his daughter off to college and a writer who'd been immersed in themes of family life, find new and original subjects to explore?

With Emma gone, how would I reorder my time? Fill those hours once claimed by my role as the Prince of Rides?

What an opportunity I had, I thought, to confront change rather than simply react to it, to shape the rest of my life.

One day, not all that far in the future, some stranger would come to this house, toss my Cape Cod watercolors and sketches into the trash, cluck and laugh about all the antiquated computer and phone lines wired into the baseboards way back in 1997.

Perhaps Jeff and his kids would patch together a memorial service for Uncle Jon and join Paula and Emma in scattering ashes up here to join those of Julius and Stanley. Maybe they'd read from an updated volume of "The Last Resort," one that I wrote myself.

CLAIMING THE MOUNTAIN

*Perhaps the book of life, in the end, is the book of
what one has lived and if one has lived nothing,
he is not in the book of life.*

—THOMAS MERTON, *A SEARCH FOR SOLITUDE*

THE MOUNTAIN PUT on a spectacular show for me
this morning. The sun fooled me by rising behind high
clouds, skipping the sunrise that usually wakes me up. I
dozed, oblivious, until seven, when crisp rays of light broke
through the sky and ringed the crest of the mountain. This
was even better than computer animation.

The pastoral atmosphere belied the fact that a struggle
was under way here, for nothing less than the soul of the
place. Having honored Lenny's memory, I'd declared war on
his taste, his drinking signs, the homilies about home and
hearth, the glasses with stenciled slogans, the general
neglect and decay inside, the Dogpatch-like grounds outside.

To each his own, but there was little in the house that
didn't seem ugly to me. And in the tiny space, the ugliness
was magnified, inescapable, suffocating.

Drawing on my rusty corporate instincts and management

skills, dormant for nearly a decade, I recruited a powerful army to help in this domestic and spiritual battle.

If I wasn't quite the all-powerful leader of this army, I was definitely its counselor, consultant, and, of course, its bankroll. I felt a strong bond with my enlistees, perhaps cemented by the fact that this was a no-holds struggle. There could be only one survivor, the house or me.

I signed up Trudy the house cleaner, a battalion all by herself. A German-born transplant who'd lived upstate for years, Trudy hated filth and clutter. When she first saw this house, she shook her head in disgust, took her shoes off, pulled a razor blade out of her purse, stepped into the bathtub, and proceeded to scrape every inch of it.

Like the men in trucks, she had a deep philosophical bent and a willingness to share her reflections. Trudy announced up front that she didn't drive in snowstorms, hewed to several idiosyncratic cleaning rituals, demanded certain tools and supplies, and as a general rule had already taken enough crap in her life and wouldn't take any more.

Twice during every cleaning session—a relentless assault that took hours—she toted her thermos of coffee outside, lit a cigarette, and sat out on the mountain for a yak. I was expected to stop my own work and join in.

Probably because Lenny was sick and hadn't spent much time here in his last couple of years, the place was a mess. The windowsills were dusted with dirt, the shag carpets smelled of dogs, spiders had claimed every corner with their webs.

I'd made sporadic efforts at dusting and vacuuming, but watching Trudy work, I understood what she meant about men and order. The first time she came, she spent six hours in the house, changing the nature of the place profoundly. She gave me the gift of cleanliness, the pleasure of living in a house that smelled good and looked orderly. She charged me twenty-five dollars.

I protested that it was too little, but she silenced me with a wave of her hand and said she'd be back.

As hard as Trudy worked, and as much of an improvement as she made, it was a dent, a drop in a bucket. I couldn't be an armchair general; I had to pitch in. Aside from well-digging and backhoeing, I didn't want my troops to do things I wasn't willing to do myself. And I wanted to learn how to take care of a house, not just hire people to do it for me. This, I supposed, was part of life without the Fool.

I believed fifty was a milestone that needed to be recognized and marked, celebrated not just as a birthday but as a passage. There was a limit to what you could do about your body wearing out, I thought. You could, however, keep your mind active and curious. I was stepping out of myself, living out of character, doing things people had never expected of me.

This, I thought, was spiritual in itself. It helped make literal age irrelevant in some ways. It was a way to stay young in the head.

I learned something new every day I spent on the mountain—about killing mice or planting gardens or stocking hummingbird feeders. And about me. As a matter of autonomy, of identity, I needed and wanted to take care of myself here.

Besides the exercise I got on rambling walks with the dogs, I'd taken up a long-dormant practice—I started run-

ning, slowly but for increasing distances, around the lake at
the foot of the mountain, sometimes up and down the mountain itself. To my sweating, huffing surprise, my body,
shocked out of its sedentary ways, was beginning to respond:
I grew thinner, felt more energetic, healthy, and virtuous.

I also needed to know how to get dust out of carpets, to
clean sinks and toilets, to keep track of ATM withdrawals.
Feeling competent was a gift I could give myself, not by what
I said or felt but by what I did.

The window shades were falling apart in my hands. I measured several and drove to hardware stores in Cambridge,
Salem, and Greenwich, trying to find replacements that fit
my oddly proportioned windows and doors. Whatever traits
Lenny and his father had as builders, uniformity was not
among them. I had to measure each window and shade
before cutting and hanging new ones.

The ancient fluorescent bulbs in the bathroom and
kitchen had blown out and needed replacing—they had to be
special ordered, of course. The railings by the doors were
falling off and had to be unscrewed and removed.

I reglued the weatherstripping dangling from the bottom
of nearly every window. I carted out boxes of yellowing newspapers. I patched holes in a score of screens.

At Jeff's suggestion—it would take ten minutes, he said—
I decided to move my office from the rear bedroom to the
larger, front one, where I could look out at the mountain. But
nothing in this house was really simple.

The king-sized bed, I discovered, was really two twins side
by side. I crawled behind them to disassemble them, but with
one turn of the screwdriver, the wooden frame cracked right

in half. The other single bed cracked even more quickly. I wanted to cry, but first I had to buy a new bed.

I scoured antique and secondhand stores for inexpensive furniture, picking up a small living room chair in Saratoga Springs, a lamp from Billy, the Shushan potter, a small table and chest from an auction.

MY NEIGHBOR DOC told me about Tim, a local schoolteacher who did lawns. Because of the drought, he was having a tough summer: nothing was growing. I didn't imagine that schoolteachers up here made a lot of money. Besides, Doc said, Tim was getting married in February; he could use the work.

The morning after I called, he pulled up in his truck with his assistant, Jason, a college student. Clean-cut, warm, soft-spoken, polite, they belonged in a Jimmy Stewart movie. One was a Yankees fan, the other loved the Mets. They told me this up front, first thing, to see where I stood.

As they checked me out, they were simultaneously taking in my abandoned-looking property. Tim whistled, then apologized, fearing he'd been impolite. He was standing by the BUS STOP display in the backyard, a sign hanging over two dilapidated benches, surrounded by chains and pulleys, presumably once used for a dog run. I explained that he couldn't be more horrified than I was.

Parts of the driveway were nearly obliterated by brush and weeds. All around the yard sat piles of firewood. A dozen or so decaying lobster traps, wagon wheels, cans, and stray pieces of wood dotted the landscape. Five or six marigolds, clearly on their last legs, sprouted wanly from what was once a garden.

The grass that remained around the house, after the predations of Joe and Chuckie, was dead, impervious to watering, battered by the drought. Dust puffed up when you walked on it, accompanied by a hollow thumping sound. The back of the house was a muddy trench, courtesy of Clarence Gould and various men in trucks. On the side a shale river, the legacy of three days of drilling, blotted out the vegetation.

I actually hadn't taken the whole picture in for a while, scrambling as I had been from one crisis to another. It was definitely a refugee scene—the war has ended, soldiers come straggling home to the abandoned village, all is in ruins.

Tim and Jason walked around the circumference of the house, a circuit accompanied by head scratching, finger pointing, murmured consultations.

"Look, I'll be honest with you," Tim said. "I don't have much work right now, and I could use some. I'm getting married next winter, and I haven't mowed a lawn since June. This place needs a lot of work. It will cost you some, but I'll clean it up for you, and at a fair price."

He didn't mention an exact amount, and I didn't press him.

"Do what you have to do," I said. "I don't have tons of money to spend. But I hate the way this place looks."

I could see that Jason and Tim were dying to take the place on. "You don't get to make so much of a difference that often," Tim told me. It was not only a job but a mission. Square foot by square foot, inside and out, I was fighting to gain the upper hand. Go ahead, I told Tim. Do it.

They arrived first thing in the morning, raking, sawing,

digging, sweating for hours in the heat, hardly ever pausing. Simultaneously, they talked baseball all day, dissecting trades, speculating about this pitcher's arm, that hitter's temperament. They were both in baseball leagues themselves and recapped each night's game.

I expected Norman Rockwell to come striding up the drive any moment, pipe in mouth, easel in hand.

Tim and Jason cleared out the brush, burned piles of leaves, carted in topsoil and mulch, pruned trees. They dug up a buried vodka stash and poured the contents down the mountain. They hauled stones from the fence that is the border of my property and created two raised gardens that wrapped around the back and side of the house.

Leaving me notes every afternoon, telling of their progress and their plans, they reseeded the lawn and covered it tenderly with straw to protect the new growth.

They worked for days, as I grew increasingly nervous about the bill. But one afternoon, returning from a run to Shushan, I drove up and was shocked to see nothing dead, dying, or unsightly around my small cabin.

The bill for ten days' work was $645. Tim presented it personally, with an apology.

I surprised myself—and him—by giving him a hug. I don't think I've ever embraced a landscaper before.

"Tim, you've transformed this place. I can't tell you how grateful I am," I burbled. "I don't see an ugly thing." That wasn't quite true: the long slope down from the front of the house was overgrown with saplings and scrub that would soon block my view, but that was too big a job for Tim. It would take a bulldozer. Still, Tim had wrought miracles.

I saw his face glow red. "Happy to do it," he said. "Glad you liked it." He wasn't just relieved about my response to the bill (probably a third of what so much work would have cost back home) but proud of his handiwork. In the next few days he brought several of his friends by to show it off.

BIT BY BIT, I made the place mine.

My Cape Cod sketches and watercolors were on the walls, my stone gargoyles in front of the fireplace. A portrait of a smiling Thomas Merton hung on one wall of my study and a poster from the movie *Ed Wood* on the other.

I bought simple vases for flowers, a new blue teapot, stoneware coffee mugs, and a cast-iron frying pan from Vermont. I replaced a sputtering faucet and finally discarded the last of the dried-flower arrangements. I had the big old antennae taken down and cleared out the shed.

I replaced each torn window shade with a crisp new one, changed the locks and distributed keys to neighbors. I tossed out the NOT YET DIVORCED sign from the kitchen. I got rid of the party line at last and added a second line for my computer.

Outside, I was seized by planting fever. One Sunday I drove into Vermont and came across a nursery selling lovely trees, shrubs, and flowers. Knowing even less about plants than I did about home renovation, I recognized very few. But I pulled the van over anyway.

The proprietress, a patient woman who didn't seem to notice that I didn't know much about gardens, talked about her plants the way gardeners do, as if they were children: this one likes water, that one isn't happy with more than five hours of sunlight. She asked a bunch of questions about where my house was, which direction the mountain faced, how much sunlight it got.

I stuffed my van with four trees, a butterfly bush—something I'd never heard of—a dozen perennials, and several flowering shrubs, along with giant blocks of peat moss and eighty pounds of cow manure.

I can't imagine what the car looked like to passersby, with a red maple protruding from one window and the branches of a Norway maple poking out of the driver's-side window behind my ear. The dogs sat sandwiched between plants and cow shit.

I had to drive the whole way home with my neck craned forward so I could see the side mirror. Pulling up the mountain, I was worried that the load would shift and either crush the dogs or blow out the back door, spewing a wide trail of manure, moss, and greenery.

When I unloaded my bounty, the afternoon sun was blinding and the air humid. Instantly sweaty, I dug holes all over the mountaintop, mixing peat moss with cow manure in alternating layers just as the garden lady had instructed, moistening my excavations with the hose, thanks to the seventy-five-foot attachment I'd bought on the way home.

Dragging trees around, moving them from spot to spot, creating a peat-moss "well" around their roots to hold water—I was obsessed. When I saw that I'd chosen some sites poorly, I dug the plants up and replanted them elsewhere.

I was stunned to look up from my labors and see that the sun was sinking. But the hole I was digging for the Norway maple wasn't yet deep enough; I'd been hampered by the roots from some dead tree.

So I ran into the kitchen for a serrated bread knife, the only tool I had for such a situation, and sawed wildly at the roots. It was, by then, pitch black; I was working by flashlight, which attracted swarms of moths and mosquitoes. My legs and arms were aching badly.

When I finished around 10:00 P.M., watering everything dutifully, I was so filthy and covered in sweat that I took my shoes and pants off. Anyone driving by would have seen a large, bald, half-dressed man watering feverishly under the stars. But on the mountaintop, blessedly, no one does drive by.

I staggered inside, stepped into the shower. There were leaves between my toes, mud and manure ground into my skin. Rivers of grime poured off me. I collapsed into bed.

When I woke up the next morning, sore all over, I threw on some shorts and a shirt and ran outside. The yard was still filled with debris—shovels, plastic plant containers, piles of dirt and random holes. But miraculously, there was a ramrod-straight red maple that would be shading the back of the house in, oh, fifteen years. In front of the bedroom window, where the sun comes blazing in at dawn, was the Norway maple, still alive.

Afterward, my daily ritual began each morning with a careful inspection of my plantings; I noted new buds and stalks, exulted at anything that grew. I watered thoroughly. I also wondered what had come over me, digging in such a frenzy, as if failing to plant that very day would mean failing to do it at all. Maybe my relationship with nature was so tenuous that I saw planting as a one-shot chance, use it or lose it. Maybe the mountain was claiming me, too.

FROM DOC, WHO called whenever there was a lightning storm to make sure I wasn't standing dumbly outside; to the vet who gently and patiently explained Julius's allergies and wanted to be called anytime, day or night; to Trudy, who worked twice as many hours as she got paid for; to the car dealer who raced up the mountain when my minivan got a rock stuck in its wheelbase; to Tim, who couldn't bear to leave my house until everything around it looked just right—people had been good to me up on this mountain, as kind as people have ever been. Was it because upstate folks were simply nicer, as I sometimes thought? Or because I'd let them help me?

It had been a while since I'd put myself in a situation where I'd met so many new people. People describe me as social and outgoing, but the truth is, I'm shy and usually wary. Psychoanalysis had turned me inward, as had taking care of Emma. And so had the battering brought on by several ugly career crises.

But I liked these people upstate, and they liked me. Not only did they give me advice, but within a few minutes, I invariably found myself giving them some too: whether or not to buy a computer and what kind, what colleges their teenagers might look into, what books to give their friends and relatives. I was amazed at how the people accepted my counsel. For whatever reason, people talked to me; it had been apparent in my early reporting days, and it was still true.

Forging a connection with people was also a spiritual experience in itself. Oddly, I hadn't seen myself as good at it. I'd had too many job scrapes, moved too many times, left too many friends behind. I talked to few strangers back home; I guarded against others' intrusion. But since coming to the mountain, I seemed to be talking to everybody—the guys at the hardware store, my fellow lunchers at the Burger Den, neighbors I encountered on the road.

These conversations not only connected me to the place, they were strangely educational, a different kind of graduate school. I was learning about food by stopping at farm markets and the local co-op. I was learning about exercise from other joggers I encountered on trails.

I never wanted to feel that I had learned enough. Change had given me this opportunity. In midlife, it's tempting to succumb to the idea that because you have more years behind you than ahead, what you already know will carry you along.

But claiming the mountain was not just about finding good help, planting maples, or hanging art, it was about learning. From Trudy, how to scrape stains off the bathtub. From Tim, how to help dying plants regenerate.

The house itself had taught me a thousand small things. It was all a drop in the large bucket of my ignorance, but I was pleased at the prospect of filling it up.

. . .

I WAS SITTING out in the Adirondack chair, hoping for a breeze to drive the flies and mosquitoes away for a few minutes, admiring my handiwork and Tim's, when the portable phone rang. Jeff was calling from yet another doctor's office.

"Guess what?" He sounded numb. "Looks like we're going to have twins."

RUN TO THE RACETRACK

It is a commonplace of moral science that absolute morality is impossible—in other words, that all men sin.

—H. L. MENCKEN, "HONOR"

WHEN ALL WAS said and done, despite bad water, rodent invasions, financial realities closing in, and lots of second thoughts, I felt celebratory for days after closing. In fact, I decided I owed myself the same kind of ritual observance I'd given Lenny, only more upbeat.

I'd spent hours poring over Merton's journals and mulling over why spirituality is so remote and inaccessible a notion to people. My conclusion was that I needed to do something joyous.

Janine, a local artist and the town of Greenwich's leading picture-framer, had been pondering the Merton portrait I brought in. She'd become curious about him and his work, so I'd given her a couple of his books. She decided that she defined spirituality this way: happiness.

She had a point. These journeys don't have to be grim, lonely, or laden. The associations with monasteries, sacred scripts, and a vengeful God make spirituality seem beyond our grasp, requiring enormous sacrifice, holiness, or isolation.

Yet for me, spiritual questing has never been in the service of dogma or doctrine. I don't pray in any traditional sense, but when I look inward, I am seeking understanding, the strength to take stock with clarity and honesty, and the courage to act on what I see—what Enlightenment philosophers called the risk of discovery.

There *is* a huge risk involved whenever you seek to discover yourself. You might find that you're not as happily married as you thought you were. That you're growing older than you've permitted yourself to acknowledge. That you have few true friends, or the wrong ones. That you're not happy with the place you're living or fulfilled by the work you're doing. That you're not happy or fulfilled, period.

Before these realizations, you might have been content to stumble along, to accept the reality of your life. Afterward, though, you face a choice—to change or not? And if the choice is change, what sort? Will you regret it? Simply pile additional mistakes onto the ones you've already made?

No wonder these notions of contemplation and change seem naturally linked to religious admonitions—the firm directions officially provided by a supreme being or a sacred text.

Perhaps if spirituality could be linked more to enjoyment of life, the fulfillment of dreams, the adventure of change and growth, it might feel—even become—less remote. This was my experiment, anyway.

Self-awareness, introspection, searches for the meaning of things—all those are hard, sometimes painful undertakings. It was important to step away sometimes and, as Merton had put it, "cast our awful solemnity to the winds."

I'm struck often at how hopeless people feel about their lives and their options. They are bound by social obligation and circumscribed by fear; they have kids, mortgages, obligations, health plans. They're slow or unable to seek help for their problems; it's too expensive or embarrassing. They're taught to be frightened of change. What if I lose what I have? What if I fail? Or am humiliated?

All these cautions and reservations are understandable, even valid. Yet the drama is that when all is said and done there's a choice—get help if needed, take risks if necessary, make changes when appropriate. In my experience, the people who do these things have more often found happiness than the people who haven't.

There are no guarantees. The good guys can lose, the risk takers stumble. But the choice—risk versus caution—looms right in front of us.

Happiness is the hope for much of what we do. If we have that, stasis is a fine option. If we don't, change and risk are sometimes the only choice.

Janine's idea about spirituality's link to happiness worked for me, and I decided to test it out.

I ran to the racetrack.

There's nothing like horse racing to teach you about the vagaries of life and fate. And few tracks are as atmospheric as the aging Saratoga Racetrack, built as a sporting playground in the last century for the millionaires who came to take the waters, now grown increasingly egalitarian, quaint, and threadbare.

The owners and swells of the horse crowd parade around the paddock with their horses before each race, as extended families from Queens sit in their lawn chairs with beer and tout sheets to make their picks before the bugler's call to post.

In the stands in the brilliant sunshine, Jeff at my elbow, my own tout sheets spread across my lap, binoculars dangling from my neck, I savored the thought of my quiet house—*my* house—waiting for me on the mountain. I was nearly aglow with spiritual warmth. There could hardly be a better way to celebrate one's fiftieth birthday, when one is, as Merton wrote, beginning to be old.

There is something delicious about going to the track; it makes you feel slightly wicked and sinful without really being either. It was a treat to see the wiseguys in shiny suits and tasseled loafers, the tanned owners in pastel sports jackets, the working stiffs who stared at TV monitors hung out on the lawn, having traveled for hours to bet on horses but never bothering to look at one.

To be here, after ruminating on the mountain, brought me back to earth; like reading Mencken, it kept my perspective in check. How holy could you feel checking out horses for foam or twitchiness?

I loved picturing the legendary gangster Meyer Lansky—credited with inventing the economics of organized crime—at Hialeah, outside Miami. The feds would be lurking somewhere in the stands as tanned men in expensive suits whispered in his ear. His bets would be extremely well informed.

At these times, I always wanted a stogie and wished I could linger a few weeks at the track to watch the workouts, hang out at the racing bars and restaurants, yak with some of the stable hands, so I could stand by the rail and gossip confidently about how red-hot Doublerose's jockey was or how Groovy Actor was a great mud horse.

Alas, I was small-time at the track, and everybody from the usher to the restaurant maître d' knew it. But if I closed my eyes for a second, I was Lansky at Hialeah in its heyday, waiting for the flight of the flamingoes to kick off the ninth race.

Yeah, I'm bad. I'd gone to the ATM down the road and withdrawn eighty dollars. I figured nine races, a five-dollar bet each race, plus parking, a Diet Coke, and a pretzel. I was a big shot, a track freak. I spent nearly as much in *Racing Forms* and tout sheets as I bet.

There was a time when I knew something about horses, but that was long ago, before marriage and mortgages. A close friend who went to the track with me in Atlantic City had gotten in deep with some rough people. His wife had thrown him out of the house, and he had lost his credit cards. He bet his last hundred dollars on a long shot.

His horse took off out of the gate as if he'd been fired from a cannon, stayed well in the lead through the three-quarter turn, then tripped over the guardrail, plunged upside down into the pond in the middle of the track, and drowned.

My friend stared in disbelief at the fate of his last hundred dollars—forty of which he'd borrowed from me—and then looked up at the sky.

"I hear you," he said abruptly, turned and left the track, never to return. This story was not only true but had a happy ending: his wife took him back, and he went on to become a top administrator at an Ivy League university.

Who says horse racing isn't spiritual?

THIS WASN'T THE only time in recent years that a visit to Saratoga Racetrack felt life-affirming.

It was a year earlier, almost to the day, that Emma and I—just three weeks after her surgery—were heading back to the camp she'd had to leave earlier that summer. It was time for the annual camp fair, and she'd promised herself and her cabin mates when she came home in July that she would return in August. Swaddled among pillows, unable to walk more than a couple of blocks, she was still in considerable pain as we headed north from New Jersey.

I was, in retrospect, much too disoriented to be making the drive. I was in shock, recovering from the indescribable trauma any parent feels when his child is subject to that kind of pain and anguish.

I wasn't functioning well. I drank cologne at a publisher's sales conference, thinking it was mouthwash, and came close to passing out when the much coveted moment came to describe a forthcoming book. I stopped at a gas station and poured gallons of gasoline down my pants leg instead of into the tank.

I was loopy, forgetful, distracted. I worried about how Emma could make it through the camp fair, staged in a hilly meadow without comfortable chairs or flat walkways.

But on the way to Vermont, driving up the New York State Thruway, we passed the signs for Saratoga—and looked at one another. "Want to go to the track?" I asked.

"You bet," she said.

What a profoundly stupid idea. A fall would have been disastrous. Her stitches had been removed days before; her body was just beginning to heal. She had little stamina. She couldn't lift anything. The parking lots at Saratoga were vast, the stands crowded.

Besides, Jeff and Michele were waiting for us. They had a comfortable ground-floor room for Emma, the bed all ready and made up. She'd get the rest she needed for the grueling day she faced at camp.

Yet the track was a great idea, too. She, Paula, and I had been through an elemental journey of the soul, if ever there was one. I doubt I'll ever experience a more spiritual moment than seeing her in the hospital recovery room, a sight that burned deeply and forever into my consciousness a sense of just what was important and what wasn't.

Fifteen minutes later we were pulling into the preferred parking lot at the track. A guard took my word for it that Emma was hurting—her discomfort was visible, even to a stranger—and let us park by the curb. Still, it was a long and difficult walk. I supported one arm and felt increasingly guilty and stupid.

Who, exactly, was I going to the track for? Her or me? The answer, I told myself, was us. It was a return to life, an affirmation. Being here would help her feel normal again, remind her that ordinary pleasures were not only possible but at hand. It was a way of showing her clearly, as well as telling her, that she would be all right. I thought Paula would beat me to death if she knew.

Across the concrete walkway, through crowds of people, onto the escalator, then unsteadily up the stairs we went. I moved ahead, arms outstretched like a Secret Service agent, clearing the way, gently nudging people aside, maneuvering around obstacles.

I saw Emma wince every time she was bumped, and thought with each step, "Dumb, dumb, dumb."

By the time we got to our seats in the grandstand, Emma was drained of color, obviously in pain. I used the pillows I'd carried to build her a nest in a chair, then trotted off for soda, pretzels, popcorn. She drank heavily but didn't eat much.

Meanwhile, she scanned the program and picked her horses; I placed the bets for her. And she won three races in a row. There is no happier person than somebody who leaves a racetrack with pockets stuffed full of other people's cash, even when that someone is recovering from spinal surgery.

A YEAR LATER, as Jeff and I pored over horse profiles and histories, Em was fine. The guard wouldn't have recognized her, so tall and straight and vibrant, healthy enough to go to Eastern Europe for five weeks on a student service project.

And I had recovered too, finally grabbing my house on the mountain, a process that had begun when she and I had visited Yokumville the previous year.

The surgery, I'd come to see, had jolted me out of my daily existence, reminded me that time was both precious and finite. Yet if I could see the tenuousness of my life more clearly, I couldn't merely flee it.

If I tried to confront change merely by leaving New Jersey to hide on a mountaintop, I wouldn't be stepping outside my life at all, simply hauling it along to a new setting. What I was after was more complicated—to move out of the world while remaining smack in the middle of it.

I wanted to write and sell books, to continue my hard work as a father and a husband, to be a good friend to the people who depended on me, to still know the pleasures of good movies, sitcoms, and books. At the same time Merton had inspired me to believe that solitude and silence were essential for anybody undertaking the hard work necessary for self-discovery and internal—spiritual, if you will—advancement.

I was trying both to remove myself from my life and to work feverishly to stay involved with it, a spiritual trick in some ways tougher than a monk's. I wanted it all. And, little by little, I thought I was getting there, seeing more, understanding better.

I knew that tragedies and shocks could be gifts as well as setbacks. That life sometimes was, in fact, an interval between sorrows, marked by journeys and experiences that deepened and altered us.

Being a spectator that afternoon, sitting in the stands and watching fate and luck played out nine times in a row, I recognized that in stepping out of my ordinary existence and going to the mountain, I had at least given myself a good seat from which to see more clearly how the diorama of life looks.

Back home, working hard, submerged in the details of a household, I, like most people, was too caught up in my own routines to see things particularly clearly, aside from the sense of wheel-spinning I'd developed.

But from my vantage point on the mountain, in the grandstand of my own life, I saw quite vividly the cycle of gain and loss, fate and luck, challenge and opportunity, that marked my life and others'.

I saw that the boundaries of those things were blurry, impossible to define. Today's bad luck was tomorrow's great chance. Doors closed and opened constantly in a funny, slam-bang, Rube Goldberg way. Neither loss nor gain ever constituted a permanent state.

Emma was moving away, toward college and independence, but I was already regaining freedom and the kind of time with and closeness to Paula that marriages only have before children come or after they leave.

I felt I'd separated from my own siblings years ago. And Paula and I might have had another child, if we hadn't ended two pregnancies after prenatal tests detected a fatal genetic disease. Nobody marks these children's deaths or wonders what their lives would have been like, except for us. Yet I could still cry over their loss as freely as if we'd lost them the day before.

Now, too young to be a grandfather but past the point of wanting more children, I was just the right age to spoil somebody else's. I'd happily drive Jeff crazy, bringing bags of toys and goodies, taking his kids to stupid movies and small-time carnivals, things I suspected Jeff and Michele would not love as much as I did.

The news that Jeff was going to be a father had already triggered profound changes in our friendship. I foresaw the loss of our incomparable bull sessions but also foresaw the opportunity to be as good a friend to him as he had been to me. If I'd fired the Fool, I wanted to promote the Helper. I couldn't live other people's lives or present myself as a font of wisdom, but I'd made enough mistakes and experienced enough failures to spot some potholes. And I could put that knowledge to use.

Few people are prepared for parenting until they do it, but Jeff was especially fuzzy. He and Michele didn't have a freezer ("We only eat natural foods," he told me) or a microwave. ("I'll never have one in my house," Michele announced.) They didn't understand why they'd need changing tables. They were both approaching forty; their lives had fallen into cherished and predictable patterns, most of which a baby— let alone two—would blow to smithereens.

I could do the thing men so rarely do for one another— serve as an affectionate mentor. I badgered Jeff into renting an inexpensive office nearby, where he could retreat when babies were screaming and he needed to write. I nagged him into buying a freezer. When he talked about an upcoming trip to Italy, I tried to explain as gently as I could that he probably wouldn't be seeing Europe this year.

Gifts to others are often gifts to oneself, and this was my experience with Jeff. I thought: I'll help him prepare for his own journey of the soul. When the children come, he will be as ready as any new father can really be. Then, to one degree or another, we'll go our separate ways, do the very different work we'd each have to do.

For myself, at fifty, I saw the beginning of distinct physical and emotional changes. I needed stronger prescriptions for my eyeglasses. I had plenty of energy, but for the first time, I sometimes needed to nap in the afternoon. Yet I also felt wiser, calmer, *nicer*.

Beginning to be free of the fear and anger and disappointment that come with intense ambition, I'd started to want different things for the balance of my life.

I would be a parent until I dropped, but my daughter would need me in different, though sometimes challenging, ways.

I wanted my writing to shine, but the fire was internal more than external. I never wanted to be a Big Shot again. I was looking ahead, not up.

Quarrels and arguments had largely vanished from my life. I was becoming less rigid and more curious, less stubborn and more open-minded. I brushed things off more frequently, turned the other cheek, looked the other way. I did less damage.

Even as we advanced relentlessly toward aging and death, we regenerated. I was facing not stasis but an ongoing rebirth. Sitting in the grandstand, watching the winners and losers, I could feel as well as see that my life wasn't moving in a straight line. No one's did.

And I had some control over how I aged.

My chosen slogan for this plunge past my fifth decade was the one motto Immanuel Kant proposed in the late 1700s for the Enlightenment: *Sapere aude*—Dare to know. Dare to take the risk of discovery, exercise the right of unfettered criticism, accept what historian Peter Gay called the loneliness of autonomy.

I planned to give it a shot. In fact, I had already begun.

But the trip to the racetrack further reminded me that if I didn't fear taking on some of the difficult questions, I also shouldn't overlook one of life's most basic tasks—to have a good time.

Sitting in the grandstand, watching the sleekly beautiful horses warm up, I decided to put five bucks on a horse that had won three of her last four races, five of her last six at this track. She was heavily favored, my trusted tout's pick of the day.

She came out of the gate last and stayed there for every foot of the six furlongs she ran. She finished so far behind the others it was almost as if she were in the next race.

Still, nobody looking over at me at that moment would have seen a trace of disappointment. Were Meyer Lansky himself sitting at a front table in the clubhouse, puffing on a giant Havana and gazing down at me, he would have seen a highly contented man. A big winner.

PRIMESTAR AND FRANKENSTEIN

One afternoon the foreman came and set up the
meter, and Merton pressed the switch and knew
the blessing of light had arrived.

—MONICA FURLONG, MERTON: A BIOGRAPHY

ONE DAY I pressed the power switch on my zapper and
I knew the blessing of old movies had come to my mountaintop, via a little satellite dish perched on the ridge overlooking
the valley.

This dish was ugly and intrusive, out of keeping with the
striking view and the spare tone I'd established here. It made
me a little queasy. I'd come all this distance to experience
solitude in a beautiful, isolated place, and here I was bringing a gazillion TV channels into a tiny cabin.

I felt like the Antichrist I have sometimes been accused of
being, by people who feel differently about technology and
culture than I do.

Merton would not have approved. He had fantasized for
years about the simplicity of life in his hermitage, about
extreme quiet and an almost primitive existence. He feared

being overcome by the loneliness that had often afflicted him, even in the monastery among his brothers.

Yet he wrote that he wanted to experience the "ordinariness" of life. He wanted to feel hunger and fatigue, heat and cold. He wanted to fill his days with humble tasks—cooking, tidying up—until he died.

Technology played no part of this, either in church lore or in monastic practice. To Merton, machinery meant noise, vulgarity, diversion. "Technology. No!" he wrote in *Dancing in the Water of Life*. "We gain nothing by surrendering to technology as if it were ritual, a worship, a liturgy . . ."

These ideas of Merton's had become very real for me on the mountaintop, where my own days were filled, for perhaps the first time in my life, in much of that traditionally spiritual way—with contemplation, nature, solitude, simplicity.

Solitude was proving an unpredictable wizard, brewing spells and spirits. One of its tricks was to appear beautiful and serene, then turn in a flash, dredging up sorrows and terrors deeply buried. I had worked so hard to forget things, only to claw my way to a place where I couldn't help remembering.

Solitude was demanding, unsparing, as unnerving and challenging as it was rewarding. The purest solitude, I came to see, had little to do with where I was, how many people were around me, or how many trucks I could hear on the highway. It was internal, only loosely related to my physical situation. It was about getting to the darkest and emptiest places inside. In fact, it was in this loneliness that the best and most important things began to happen.

As for self-reliance, which to Merton meant taking responsibility for his life by reducing it to its simplest and most essential tasks, it was something I'd never achieved back home in my other existence, where a small army of people did things for me, kept even my modest life running.

Here on the mountain, though, I'd tasted autonomy. I was living as close to a cloistered, monklike existence as I ever had or would, walking the dogs, tending my new garden, working. I bought and prepared my own food, kept the house tidy, did my laundry at the coin-op in town, hired plumbers and electricians.

This meant a lot to me.

For Merton, autonomy, spirituality, and solitude were intertwined, all links in the same evolutionary spiritual chain. Technology was merely a raucous intrusion, distasteful and frivolous, something that interfered with contemplation, introspection, and, thus, faith. Thoreau would have enthusiastically agreed.

Such suspicions of technology are almost synonymous with morality in modern thought. It's hard to find philosophers or ethicists who celebrate faxes, the Internet, or halogen lamps.

When I ran to this mountain, I found I had leaped back a decade or two in terms of technology. Picking up a newspaper meant driving four miles. I didn't have a working TV or radio. Then there was that pesky party line. People kept asking me if it was wonderful to be so unwired. "You'll realize that the Internet can't compete with the woods," one writer advised.

I understood the script I was expected to follow. Here in this beautiful place, my latent sense of spirituality and love of nature awakened, the script called for me to renounce technology and revel in the silence and solitude—and of course, to a great extent I did.

But technology itself was never really the issue. Our raging media, political, and academic debates about technology are bounded by ideologues, moralists, and extremists—Luddites who want to turn the clock back, Internet utopians who've made technology a new religion, the Unabomber and moral guardians all invoking technology or people's fear of it for their own purposes.

Their impact is a testament to how frightening change is. Reflexively, we see technology as a threat and a menace; we have to work to see that it is also sometimes an opportunity or a blessing.

For me, the issue is nearly always balance—finding a middle way to take advantage of technology's very real benefits without allowing it to intrude too greatly.

This middle way didn't involve either mindlessly embracing new gadgetry or railing about technology's evils. It meant finding a way of living that enjoyed what was convenient, connecting, or entertaining about technology, protecting at the same time the quiet necessary for reflection and self-awareness.

The point of all these backdrops—my Primestar and computer-equipped cabin on the mountain, the splendor of the mountain and valley vistas outside it—was to help me answer questions I'd come here to answer. Who am I? What am I about? Who do I want to be?

Technology is incidental to this. Computers and TV's have no more (or less) to do with it than trees and birds do. None of these things can define us, bound our identity, shape our souls.

Every one of us, Merton wrote, is shadowed by an illusory person, the man or woman we want to be but often can't be or aren't.

On the mountain the challenge was to dig down to my essential self, in just the way Clarence dug for water. To find it, recognize and acknowledge it, then struggle to reconcile that person with the person I wanted to be.

It's an isolating experience, an invisible process, hard to explain to busy people preoccupied with the dramas of their own lives. Thus it is inherently lonely, even in less solitary surroundings than mine here.

The isolation wasn't purely wonderful; it was also disorienting and disconnecting. Life was out of balance, just as it would be if I were on-line all day or watched TV compulsively. I appreciated being less wired but not having the plugs pulled. Being out of touch—with friends, my on-line communities, research, and discussions, movies and *The X Files*—was also a loss.

I thought both extremes out of whack. To be hooked up to the Net and cable round-the-clock, with faxes and phones warbling, was unhealthy; it precluded reflection and meditation. To be cut off altogether was to take the cloister walk, leave the world behind. And I liked the world.

Still, I felt guilty, almost dirty, watching the Time Warner technician dig a hole and plant a four-foot Primestar satellite dish at the left-most slice of my valley view. A half dozen times I wanted to tell him to stop.

He had wanted to plunk the thing down right in the middle of my lawn, but I wouldn't let him. He was shocked at my balkiness. This would give you the clearest reception, he said. I held firm.

In fact, I almost called him back to take the thing away. I feared I was missing a chance to take a big spiritual leap forward. Up here, I was supposed to do what Thoreau and Merton did.

Well, perhaps not Merton, not entirely.

FOR ALL HIS dislike of technology—most of which, as a Trappist, he was forbidden anyway—Merton was delighted when electricity came to his hermitage in 1965. One of his brothers had wired up a stove and lights for him; Merton was thrilled to be able to read at night.

The year before, Merton had been similarly delighted with the kerosene lamp he found awaiting him in a paper bag on his desk after mass. It filled the hermitage with a mysterious light, but it smoked a lot, he discovered, and was hard to read by.

A few months later, in midwinter, he tried out a Coleman lamp, a great improvement. "Beautiful lamp," he wrote. "It burns white gas and sings viciously but gives out a splendid green light in which I read Philoxenos, a sixth-century Syrian hermit."

It turned out he was a movie freak as a kid, too. "Why did we ever go to all those movies?" he asked ingenuously in one of his books. "And most of them were simply awful. . . . Yet I confess a secret loyalty to the memory of my great heroes: Chaplin, W. C. Fields, Harpo Marx."

In the summer of 1997 I was thrilled to sit down with my Primestar switcher and watch *Buffy the Vampire Slayer,* or call up *Scream* on a movie channel at midnight and experience the special tickle of a campy horror film on a mist-shrouded mountain with no neighbors within earshot.

I was happy, too, to finally be able to hook up to the Internet each morning, read the news, and sort through my E-mail from around the globe.

Just as Merton's hermitage grew steadily more livable, so my cabin had gotten more comfortable, reflecting the way I wanted to live, the particular mental ecology I sought.

Were spirituality and Primestar incompatible? Did one preclude the other, or could they coexist? Could I be a moral person, spend part of my life on a mountain, and still stay up late watching *The Silence of the Lambs*?

Frankly, I loved Primestar, lost wretch that I was. What mortal wouldn't? It supplied a hundred channels, all beaming in clear as window glass. There was even an old-quiz-show channel. I could order up half the movies in the world every night, watch reruns of almost every TV show I ever loved.

On the mountain I often fantasized about yakking with Merton, talking to him about the middle options, a life between his isolated existence and my overcrowded one. I pictured calling him up, telling him to drive over for a drink. Then we'd sprawl in my little living room with low-fat microwave popcorn to watch *High Noon,* available for pennies just by punching in a password.

Would this have come between Merton and God? What kind of deity would disapprove of old World War II movies? Would it have clouded Merton's contemplation? Or maybe eased some of his loneliness and fear, as it had for me?

Technology is neutral, I would have told him. It brings nothing to the table but the box it came in. It is a tool, like a hammer or saw. Science and technology are amoral, capable of both great good and monstrous evil.

But people weren't neutral, of course; we did have morals and we could make choices. We could use technology to whatever ends we wished. It had as much or as little morality as we provided in the way we integrated it into our lives.

We could find a balance between an overload of technology and an undersupply.

The greatest technomorality drama of all time, the book I most wish I had written, remains *Frankenstein,* Mary Shelley's timeless warning about unthinking practitioners of new technology and the horrors they could unleash.

This dense Gothic novel was one of the first great literary broadsides against advancing technology and the blind way in which we embrace, then recoil from it. The story of the monster and the scientist who made him is a dramatic portrait of the tremendous unease that accompanies new technology.

It was still striking on many levels as I incorporated it into my mountaintop reading—noticing, for the first time, that the only character in the novel who thought about technology, responsibility, and morality at all was the monster.

Shelley got right to the point on her title page, which included a quotation from Milton's *Paradise Lost:*

> *Did I request thee, Maker, from my clay*
> *To mould me man? Did I solicit thee*
> *From Darkness to promote me?*

Frankenstein wasn't the horror story that popular culture had broadcast so often but a philosophical morality tale about the dangers of creating things without sufficient care.

As Victor Frankenstein rushed to bring his creature to life, he never mulled the implications, let alone took responsibility for the monster he'd patched together. Technology, to Victor, was merely a barrier to break. "The world was to me a secret which I desired to divine," he confided. He didn't care what happened afterward.

Happy to have made the monster, Frankenstein then abandoned his creation and sent it into the world without a thought for how it would survive. He was flabbergasted when the creature returned to demand that his maker do the right thing.

Frankenstein responded by threatening to kill this bastard child he regretted engineering, wishing only that the creature go away and leave him to his former happy life.

The monster, in many ways a far more moral being, was deeply wounded and replied: "You propose to kill me. How dare you sport thus with life? Do your duty towards me, and I will do mine towards you and the rest of mankind. If you will comply with my conditions I will leave them and you at peace; but if you refuse, I will glut the maw of death, until it be satiated with the blood of your remaining friends."

Despite this hard bargaining, the monster tried to tell Frankenstein that he wasn't unreasonable. He simply wanted to be part of the human community he observed around him, and in whose company, through no conscious choice of his own, he found himself.

All the monster needed—all any technology requires—was to have the people who made and used it take responsibility for its morality and think about how it would be employed.

Considering *Frankenstein*, it seemed clear that the power of the story wasn't in the machines Victor had built or the creature he had patched together, but in this scientist's utter lack of self-awareness and self-discovery. Since Victor had no idea who he was or what he was about, his inventions inevitably spun beyond his control.

Rereading *Frankenstein*, I noticed how far we'd traveled—from nineteenth-century England to millennial America—and how strangely unenlightened we'd remained. When it came to integrating technology into our lives and our families', we were still unthinking and perplexed. No wonder we kept running back to God for simpler answers.

"So the whole question comes down to this: can the human mind master what the human mind has made?" asked the philosopher Paul Valéry.

That was the question for Frankenstein, and for me. Could I control what I'd brought to the mountain with me?

Could I go on-line on my own terms, controlling the time I spent there? Could I allow myself to sometimes feel frightened and alone, keeping my fingers off the Primestar switcher, forcing myself to think through what I was frightened about? Could I keep the sense of space around me that I so much wanted to find here?

I thought I could and should. Getting lost in technology felt as extreme and unsatisfying as running away from it.

So each day, I experimented with the balance. I went on-line in early morning, then again at the end of my workday, but not in between and never for longer than a half hour or so. I let E-mail collect, responding at my leisure. In between, I made time for quiet, for reading, for walks.

I didn't turn Primestar on before 9:00 or 10:00 P.M., if at all, and only when the chores were done, my writing finished, the dogs walked. It distracted and relaxed me, reconnected me with the world, helped my mind cool down for sleep, reminded me of watching TV at home with my family. I doubted this could be an unhealthy thing.

I could retreat to the mountain and remain well informed, stimulated, connected to my friends and family. Working out the details might take a while, but I would manage. More was at stake than E-mail.

THE MORE ELEMENTAL and, for one turning fifty, timely issue is the attitude toward change. That's what technology is the proxy for.

People who dread and fear change have little hope for the future, no faith in anything new. They value mostly what is and was. They mistrust the young, belittling them, dismissing them and their inferior values and tastes because they invariably signal change. They cling to the old, not wanting to lose what they know or relinquish their right to set agendas—but the old can't make them happy either, because they see it as constantly imperiled.

You hear such voices all the time in our culture. They scold and caw like crows in trees, squawking about all the junk on TV, the filth on the Internet, the garbage in bookstores, that awful music blaring on the radio. Implicit in the lament is the conviction that what used to be was better, purer, more substantial than what is or—God forbid—what comes next. Technology is one of the greatest menaces, the one that enables so many others.

These fearful people aren't necessarily old in chronological terms, but they are old in their attitudes, their values. They are unhappy at the prospect of having to learn new things.

I am more comfortable with change.

I see it as creative, challenging, stimulating, and exciting. I see it as generally improving a future I mean to take part in.

While I permit myself some optimism, I don't jettison every valued tradition. I welcome some change without having to embrace all of it. I can pick and choose, the slogan of the Middle Way.

I can go on-line and still read *The Seven Storey Mountain.*

My daughter can watch *Seinfeld* and still be a moral being prepared for the world.

I can walk in the woods but also drive to the movies.

I can go to a mountaintop and there, after long summer days of simplicity and thoughtfulness, click on Primestar.

THE LONELY ONE

I'll sleep alone all of my life.

—FROM THE FOLK SONG "SILVER DAGGER"

LIKE MERTON, I was both drawn to loneliness and frightened by it. Unlike him, I could and did enter and leave it at will. I could drive into Shushan to visit Billy the potter, to the Agway to schmooze about lawns, down the road to see Jeff, or back to New York City to meet Emma at JFK's international-arrivals terminal after her community-service project in Eastern Europe.

But when I returned to the mountain, I crossed an old boundary into a place, however beautiful, where loneliness reigned.

I was a veteran of loneliness; I knew how to survive it. It was so familiar it was comforting, almost like going home. At the core, loneliness was not a state someone like me—or Merton—ever really left for long, no matter where we lived.

In 1963, after years of pestering and pleading, Merton finally won permission from his abbot to spend some time in the hermitage his Trappist brothers had built for him, deep in the woods near Gethsemani.

The hut he christened Mount Olivet was numbingly cold in winter and hot in summer, initially without amenities like electricity or plumbing. Going to the bathroom outdoors in the dead of a freezing night was in itself a revelatory experience, Merton wrote to friends.

Nevertheless, he began going to Mount Olivet to read and write most afternoons, then arranged to spend an entire day there once a week. He eventually received permission to remain overnight, and wrote in his journal that he slept well for the first time in years.

In my own hermitage, I was reading not only Merton's essays, letters, and journals but several of the biographies that chronicled his dramatic, foreshortened life. It was a sobering, even sad process.

At fifty, Merton was giving birth to himself one more time, heading off on another journey of the soul. But this trip sounded sorrowful. In fact, his biographer Monica Furlong entitled the chapter that examined this period "The Lonely One."

Merton frequently described living in the woods as a powerful necessity. He wrote in his journal: "I get out of bed in the middle of the night because it is imperative that I hear the silence of the night, alone, and, with my face on the floor, say psalms, alone, in the silence of the night. It is necessary for me to live here alone without a woman, for the silence of the forest is my bride and the sweet dark warmth of the whole world is my love, and out of the heart of that dark warmth comes the secret that is only heard in silence, but it is the root of all the secrets that are whispered by all the lovers in their beds all over the world."

This was vintage Merton, the best-selling spiritual seer known to millions across the globe. Suffused with passion, his writing was an eloquent testimonial to the power of faith.

Readers encountered this stirring, holy prose and felt envy, wonder, and, in my case, a spiritual shallowness. Could his life have seemed more peaceful and purposeful? Could mine have been more mundane or barren by comparison?

Yet there was a dissonance in Merton's writing that became more pronounced, and surprising, as I pored over more of his work—usually spreading it out on the rickety picnic table outside that Lenny and his uncle had built—and considered his life.

This was the public Merton. There was another, one who wrote with a different tone and sensibility, to be found in the letters he sent his friends and in his recently published journals.

The other Merton was sometimes an angry, tortured, and unhappy man. As lovely as some of his spiritual imagery was, I found myself asking some hard questions about the messages implicit in that awe-inducing paragraph. Living alone in the woods, sometimes reading aloud from Merton's journals just to hear the sound of a human voice, I could not have had a more vivid perspective.

Was it really necessary to live alone in the woods? All the time? Did the silence of the forest really make a satisfactory bride? Was the "sweet dark warmth of the whole world" a substitute for individual human love? If so, this was a deeply troubled marriage.

I loved the silent forest, but I missed my own warm bride and the child we'd raised together. Without them it often felt a bit bleak up on the mountain, even on brilliant days.

Like Merton, I understood the chilling symbolism of beginning to be old, the critical need to mark the half-century with something deeper than dinner out or a gift certificate.

But there we diverged, profoundly. If he needed to seek God in solitude, I needed to explore spirituality with people. I found it in watching Jeff get ready for fatherhood, in helping Emma prepare for college, in weeping with an old friend while she struggled to survive the death of her beloved partner.

For both Merton and me, however, approaching fifty was dramatic stuff. The questions at stake were nothing less than how to live our remaining years, seize our remaining opportunities, chart the next set of explorations, come to some sort of reckoning with both the past and future. It also meant, for me, taking some of my last and best shots at self-discovery and, to put it more directly, choosing how to die.

As with so many other boomers, death was suddenly in the air around me, the consciousness of mortality emerging as parents, older friends and mentors, and the first of my peers began to falter and fall. I was writing my own history. I wanted immortality, though not in the conventional religious sense. I wanted to live on in the fond memories of the people I left behind, to be recalled as a supportive father, a loving husband, a devoted friend, a man who struggled to be a good person.

During the normal course of life, people like me rushed past these monumental questions, understandably too pressured or distracted to spend much time raising, let alone answering, them. Now I had given myself a rare opportunity: to stop, step back, and confront as many of these issues as I could. To live a considered, examined life.

The remainder of my days didn't have to constitute an inexorable rush toward aches, pensions, and retirement. How to spend them was my choice, and only mine. Shame on me if I didn't make the most of them.

This idea echoed through my thoughts: people who can't or won't take the time to consider their lives are fated to lose control over the nature of the years they have before them.

One morning on the mountain, staring at distant birds with Stanley and Julius as the sun exploded across the valley, I came upon an anthem in Merton's book *Seeds of Contemplation*: "Every moment and every event of every man's life on earth plants something in his soul. For just as the wind carries thousands of invisible and visible winged seeds, so the stream of time brings with it germs of spiritual vitality that come to rest imperceptibly in the minds and wills of men."

Nothing seemed truer. I'd come to the mountain to plant some new seeds in the final chapters of my life, to nourish them, and to reinvigorate myself.

Merton had chosen to do this by loving only God. I chose to do it by loving people in a better way. For me, people *were* the seeds; without them, life, faith, and spirituality became lonely, distant, and abstract, the way they seemed to have become for Merton.

MERTON'S LETTERS DURING this period revealed an exasperation both with his order and with members of his own monastery.

In the early sixties, he called himself "in effect a political prisoner at Gethsemani. A prisoner of my own inability to act, which I have strengthened a million times over by putting my life in the hands of—this Abbot. He is committed before all else to the smothering of any least spark of freedom, of political conscience, of a socially productive spirituality."

It was impossible to read his letters or journals, which had been edited and were thus more discreet, and not wonder if Merton's passion to reach the seclusion of Mount Olivet wasn't as much an effort to get away from Gethsemani and his painful battles with his abbot.

Apart from angst and loneliness, Merton's letters also disclosed a surprising number of physical ailments—bursitis, a displaced disk in his spine, poor digestion, painful skin problems. Convalescing from back surgery in Louisville in 1965, he was given permission to listen to records and was mesmerized by Bob Dylan and by Joan Baez's rendition of the folk ballad "Silver Dagger," which concluded, "I'll sleep alone all of my life."

Merton harbored a definite countercultural streak, and the turmoil of the sixties made him still more restless. Even Catholic priests had some freedom to come and go. One of his closest friends was the antiwar activist/priest/poet Daniel Berrigan, whom Merton considered heroic and with whom he corresponded regularly. Merton, too, was becoming passionately opposed to the Vietnam War, increasingly angry about what he saw as church silence on the conflict, and itchy to leave the monastery to lobby for peace, something he was repeatedly denied permission to do.

But Berrigan's kind of vocation wasn't an option for Merton. Trappists, men who live austere and rigidly circumscribed lives in small, hardworking, silent communities, devote their existence to God. The monks are supposed to exercise no exterior ministry—no preaching, teaching, lecturing, or publishing of best-sellers.

Thus Merton was already suspect. If any monk didn't need more trouble, it was he. But he got a lot more, perhaps the most heartrending of his monastic life.

In 1965, during his hospitalization, he suffered greatly both in physical and emotional ways: he fell in love with a young nurse identified by biographers only by initials such as "S." A Catholic, S. had read and been moved by Merton's work and was eager to talk to him about it. The two had a clandestine, doomed romance, an impossible encounter for a monk whose suspicious abbot was already keeping close watch on him.

Merton asked S. to write to him in an envelope marked "Conscience Matter," which meant it wouldn't be censored at the monastery. He met with her on subsequent hospital visits and borrowed money from friends so that he could take her to lunch. He called her repeatedly from Gethsemani itself, a reckless act, since conversations were bound to be overheard by one of the brothers manning the monastery switchboard.

Although engaged to a much younger man, S. told Merton she loved him in return. At least one of his closest friends and conspirators warned that he was at risk of destroying himself.

Once again, Merton had placed himself in an impossibly contradictory position. He was trapped, writes Furlong, "endlessly scheming how to talk to S. on the telephone or in person, fantasising at times about marriage, yet also striving to pursue the life of monk and hermit as if nothing had happened."

It was impossible not to feel enormous empathy. After years of abstinence, the sexual and emotional longing for a woman must have been overwhelming.

For many men, this would be called a midlife crisis. For a Trappist living under constant supervision, eager to take up the life of a hermit, it suggests another kind of agony—a profound conflict between the life he had publicly and enthusiastically chosen and what was clearly a tremendous yearning for love. The silence of the forest, his affair indicated, was not a fulfilling bride.

This was a nightmare from which there was really no good outcome possible. Either Merton had to give up the love he seemed to desperately need, or the world's most intriguing monk had to renounce the choices he'd made about life and faith.

Merton's affair was reported, as he must have known it would be, and he was summoned before his chief tormentor. The abbot told him gently but firmly that the relationship had to stop. Merton and S. had a series of poignant farewells by phone and in person, and S. left Louisville. As far as is known, the two never met or spoke again.

Merton had experienced five months of pain and joy, and now it was over.

He left the temporal world symbolically again, this time for good. In September of 1965, he made a permanent commitment to live as a hermit.

"Here I sit in the big silences and nothing speaks but the

gas heater which clucks and chunks but gives out the big heat," Merton wrote his friend Robert Lax, "for because of the bursa and the bump I no longer chop the log or fell the pine. I just sit here looking at the snow and wishing hard for some whiskey but there is none. I live a flawed existence. I am utterly without rapport."

In *Learning to Love,* the sixth volume of Merton's journals, published in 1997, he acknowledged the affair, writing about it at considerable length. His relationship with S., he wrote, was one of the most powerful and painful experiences of his life.

Though he claimed to love the young nurse as much as he had ever loved anything, he insisted that leaving Gethsemani to be with her was always an impossibility.

In a brutal but perhaps prescient journal entry, he also wondered if the relationship—he said it was never consummated—was his last chance to alter the reality of his life.

"You should have had the courage to throw everything overboard and simply go and live with her. You should have gambled on love, and you would have won. As it is, you are stuck with a futile and absurd existence in which besides *knowing* your failure and your ambiguities, you will now spend the rest of your life manufacturing alibis."

Sitting on my drafty, bug-infested porch late one summer night on the mountaintop, flanked by the eternally companionable Julius and Stanley, looking up from time to time at the moonlight-drenched valley in front of me, sifting through these journals by the light of an ancient lamp with a moth-eaten shade, I felt the enormous poignance of this man. I had come to the mountain in part to avoid spending the rest of my life manufacturing alibis.

The following fall, Merton and the Catholic theologian Rosemary Radford Ruether began a dramatic, touching correspondence, which continued until his death. Ruether, having read much of Merton's work, seemed to sense the many conflicts roiling inside him and sharply challenged his acceptance of Catholic dogma, his reasons for staying a Trappist, and his decision to remain at Gethsemani. She seemed to sense the two Mertons, the joyous monk and the tortured man.

Ruether was far more blunt about these issues than other friends had been; as a result, his letters to her were also more frank. Though Merton's spiritual brooding and frustration with monastic and church politics does filter through in his journals, his most jarring writing—expressing fierce anger and doubt about remaining in the monastery—was reserved for his many letters to friends.

Merton wrote Ruether that she was a theologian he could trust. "And I do think I need the help of a theologian. Do you think you could help me once in a while?"

What a lonely plea. I couldn't help wondering whether Merton trusted Ruether above the other theologians he enthusiastically corresponded with precisely because she saw so clearly what the others didn't and called him on the profound contradictions beween his public writings and private thoughts.

Merton wrote Ruether that he sometimes wondered if the church was real at all. "I believe it, you know. But I wonder if I am nuts to do so. Am I part of a great big hoax?"

He also had, he wrote Ruether, a "monumental" struggle with monasticism. He'd withdrawn into the deepest woods he could find, only to feel even more alienated from his order, his abbot, his church, and his faith. "I am a notorious maverick in the Order and my Abbot considers me a dangerous subject always ready to run off with a woman or something, so I am under constant surveillance. If I am allowed to live in a hermitage it is theoretically because this will keep me more under wraps than otherwise."

On the last day of that painful year, Merton wrote in his journal his expectations for 1966. "What will next year bring? I expect more sickness. . . . Less writing—more thought—more meditation and reading. . . . I want to go now and prepare a good book on prayer. But I have no real plans, except to live and free the reality of my life and be ready when it ends and I am called to God. Whenever that may be. *Deus misereatur nostri et benedicat nobis!* [God have mercy on us and bless us!]"

So Merton not only had declared himself to be "beginning to be old" at fifty, but was preparing himself for death, his move to the hermitage clearly, in his mind, the last stop. Why so gloomy a feeling in an intellectually vigorous, much loved man, who, even a generation ago, could have reasonably expected to live for decades?

Coming to a cabin in the woods was a compelling, healing necessity for me, too. Like Merton, I was feeling that a part of me was being suffocated back home. I didn't come here to get old or die, though; I saw one of the best, freest, and most exciting parts of my life as just getting under way. I wanted to prepare for it.

Still, armed with foot-high stacks of his writings, I sometimes felt as though Merton and I were here together. If you
can know a person by his writing, then it's possible to know
Merton intimately, since he wrote obsessively and frankly
almost every day of his life.

Within hours of settling in here, I understood his love of
the woods—the quiet, the birds, the beauty. I began to see
the connection so many good writers make between nature
and spirituality. I got a clearer sense of why all those artists
and poets head for Vermont or the starkly beautiful dunes
outside Provincetown.

A lifelong child of the crowded Northeast, I had never had
space, quiet, or physical beauty constitute an integral part of
my life, except during brief vacations. I saw that I needed
them. Every cliché I'd ever read about nature lifting the soul
and touching the spirit was ringing true.

Yet only partly true. By itself, the woods, the beauty, the
peace were incomplete, an important part of a life, a striking
backdrop for a life, but not life itself. After just a few weeks
here, I found that this place seemed to work best in conjunc-
tion with another sort of existence, each environment an
antidote to the other.

The way I felt closest to Merton here wasn't particularly
spiritual. I connected as a lonely one, encountering another.
He had accepted this painful part of his life, even, perhaps,
surrendered to it. I had fought it—was still fighting it—tooth
and claw.

Because I felt such kinship with him, I found myself
shocked and shaken that someone I'd turned to at so many

points in my life was emerging as someone who needed so much help himself—and never got it.

AS THE SUN climbed and the morning mists melted away, the day was cool and crystalline. I was sitting at the picnic table with a stack of journals and Merton biographies, at least a dozen books, piled around me. The sun was intense and the bugs brazen, but there was no place inside the cramped cabin to spread out all these papers and books. One of my rodent adversaries had already nibbled vengefully at the binding of one of Merton's journals, *Turning Toward the World,* and various ants and spiders had found his volumes a congenial place to gather.

Julius and Stanley, having mastered the art of looking regal without actually doing much, sat nearby like bookends, fixated on a circling hawk above the valley.

As the three of us stared out at the mountain, as I so often found myself doing, I fell into a reverie.

In my daydream, the dogs barked; a Jeep had pulled up the narrow dirt road and into the driveway. Then they wagged their tails as if discovering that the visitor was someone they knew. I wondered if it was the plumber arriving to fix my faucet, Jeff wanting to make sure we were alive after another night of power outages, or Doc stopping by to discuss the dip in our common driveway that might need leveling.

Instead, the visitor was the last person in the world I expected to see, at least partly because he'd been dead for thirty-one years.

Thomas Merton rounded the corner of the house, the dogs rushing over to greet him as an old friend.

He gripped my hand firmly, his hands encased in the cotton gloves he often wore because of his painful skin condition. He was trim and muscular, his receding gray hair closely cropped, his eyes—as in photographs his most striking feature—wise and mischievous. His face was instantly familiar from the covers of his books, his expression wise and friendly but also somewhat expectant, like a boy about to pull a prank. I remembered reading how he taught hapless novitiates at Gethsemani to hand-sign obscenities they thought were greetings.

He patted my dogs, took a seat in the Adirondack chair. He took in the view—the mountain, the tiny specks of cows in the valley, the hawk. Of course, he understood exactly why I was here. He went into the woods to be closer to God, but could you ever get closer to God than on top of a mountain? Wouldn't he have loved plunking his Mount Olivet down right here?

At many moments when I was younger, I thought of asking Merton for help, in the way that he turned to Rosemary Ruether. Mine was not one of the letters he responded to. Reading more about his life, I'd come to understand this. He got thousands of such appeals, and although he struggled for years to answer them, he finally had to give up, harassed by the effort of responding to so many strangers, many seeking charity.

In my letter, written as I was entering a Providence high school, I told Merton that I had read *The Seven Storey Mountain* at least a half dozen times.

I confided that things were lonely for me, and that I was worried about my sister. I asked if he had any thoughts about my converting to another faith, perhaps even becoming a monk. I was disenchanted with the Judaism practiced by my family, finding it oppressive, ritualistic, and empty. I told him that the idea of leaving the world behind and entering a simple life of prayer, exercise, and contemplation seemed a great thing.

Like many people, I was transfixed by his retelling of his final arrival, after several tentative false starts, at Gethsemani after a long train trip, cab ride, and walk to the gates of the monastery.

I don't even have to look it up. I know it by heart.

In the middle of the night, Merton rang the bell at the gate. After some time, the window of the gatehouse opened, and Brother Matthew looked out.

"Hullo, Brother," Merton said.

Brother Matthew recognized the visitor from his first visit and glanced at his suitcase. "This time have you come to stay?" he asked.

"Yes, Brother, if you'll pray for me," Merton said.

"That's what I've been doing," said Brother Matthew, "praying for you." Merton walked through the gate and left the world behind.

This was a fable of complete acceptance I could lose myself in. If Merton had replied and told me to come, that he was praying for me to show up, I would have been on the next train.

Sitting in my room in Providence, friendless, frightened, my sister falling apart one room away, alone most of the time with my tropical fish, I read *The Seven Storey Mountain* and could almost smell the serenity, the satisfaction and purpose that rose from every page. I wanted the love of God and the peace of a monastery.

I was a kid, of course, with no notions of disappointment, aging, or monastic or other politics. With no center of gravity of my own, I was a sucker for everybody else's. I wanted to be a Hardy boy. I wanted to be Clarence Darrow thundering at William Jennings Bryan. I wanted to be lawyer Joseph Welch bringing Joe McCarthy down to size. I wanted to be almost everybody but me.

But I didn't go to Gethsemani because Merton didn't write, because I was too young, because I could never have left my sister, because I had no money. I was later embarrassed at even having written, picturing Merton rolling his eyes at yet another plea from a tormented teenager looking for a way out of a lonely life.

Now I'm stunned to realize that as I'm turning fifty and beginning to be old, I've never been happier. What kind of a script calls for my winding up happier than Merton, decades after my richest fantasy was to be him?

How had the wise monk who symbolized direction in life lost his way while an uneducated, troubled wretch like me appeared to have found mine? I had turned to Merton for help when, I absurdly imagined on this mountain, he might have needed mine.

Thus, the fantasy that he'd turned to me for help, the way he'd turned to Ruether. It was a stretch, but it was possible.

On the mountain, all things were possible. Hummingbirds breakfasted three feet from where I did; lightning streaked across the sky and struck a few feet away. A visit from Merton—let's say he borrowed a friend's Jeep—wasn't so improbable.

Merton looked tanned, his face weathered and lined from all that monkish work outdoors, vigorous-looking despite his many physical problems. He wore a work shirt and chinos. I offered him a glass of Glenlivet and, in honor of the visit, took one myself so that he wouldn't feel uncomfortable.

Sipping from the whiskey he often pined for, he took a liking to Julius, who as a profoundly spritual creature bonded with him right away.

Merton stared for a long time at the forested peaks across the valley. He had time to visit, I was relieved to see; he wasn't a famous man stopping by to shake hands but a friend making time to shoot the breeze.

Our conversation, far from the torments and pain of his monastery, was unhurried. There was no abbot to interfere or to quarrel with; Merton was free. He turned to me with the radiant smile that seemed permanently etched on his face in almost every photograph I'd seen. He spoke quietly, formally: *It happens that you are, for some reason, a person I trust. And I think I need a person I can trust. Do you think you could help me once in a while? I do not intend to be very demanding of your time, but I would like to feel that I can resort to you for suggestions and personal advice.*

I believe in God. But I'm not sure I belong in a monastery. I'm not sure about swearing allegiance to the church. I'm not sure that faith is defined as precisely as I used to define it. I want more of a balance in my life. I want to travel and to speak freely. I want to track down S. and be with her. Having tasted

*love again, I know I need it. I don't really want to sleep alone
the rest of my life; I wonder if I have to. Should I stay at Gethsemani? Or am I long past the point of leaving, rejoining the
world, reclaiming my life? Can I still find love? Is it too late?*

He was flushed, embarrassed, especially by the part
about S.

I said I would be happy to help in any way I could. I had
spent years of my life as a Lonely One, which brands you a
Lonely One for life. The loneliness always lives right below
the surface, rising up at odd times.

So I know just how courageous your run to the mountain
was, I told him. Then I took a deep breath.

*It's presumptuous of me to say this, since I could barely keep
a job, but you should have left Gethsemani years before you
went to the hermitage. You wanted to travel. You wanted to
write freely. You wanted to love. You said yourself you were a
political prisoner, a person without real community, a member
of a church you weren't sure was even real. Those were your
words.*

*You had great doubts about religion; they're all over your
letters, journals, diaries, and books.*

*You went into Gethsemani filled with clarity and passion
and became a walking paradox. You want to be a hermit, but
you're usually writing three books at a time and cranking out
letters to half the writers in North America.*

*You say you need to be closer to God, yet you doubt, day by
day, the nature of the church's relationship to the rest of the
world. You profess blind faith in and allegiance to Christ, yet
you refuse to accept the wisdom, authority, or sincerity of your
abbot, with whom you've warred for years. I can't help won-*

dering about all the physical suffering, too. These days, we link a lot of problems like severe back pain to stress.

And why, at fifty, do you feel so old? Is it because everyone in your immediate family died young? Or because you live in pain? I was touched and troubled by a letter you wrote a relative in 1965 listing your ailments: "An arthritic hip; a case of chronic dermatitis on my hands for a year and a half (so that I have to wear gloves); sinusitis, chronic ever since I came to Kentucky; lungs always showing up some funny shadow or another on ex-rays (though not lately); perpetual diarrhea and a bleeding anus; most of my teeth gone; most of my hair gone; a chewed-up vertebra in my neck which causes my hands to go numb and my shoulder to ache—and for which I sometimes need traction."

For a man living in the country, eating well, exercising daily, and supposedly loving your vocation, finding love and warmth deep in the woods, something seems wrong. You wrote yourself that a monk's plain diet and the physical labor of monastic life is ordinarily enough to keep a man healthy for long years, that "monks traditionally die of old age." Yet you seem so certain that you won't.

You don't live in silent devotion to God. You speak loudly and often. You have not left the world beyond; you are profoundly engaged with it. No wonder you feel torn. You are not a hermit but a spiritual celebrity. Nor are you a prisoner, a man unable to act. The same will and passion that drove you into the monastery can get you out. You have earned and are entitled to the freedom you seek. And think how many hands will reach out to help you.

As I read your letters, you seem lost. You wrote that life in a Cistercian monastery is a life of prayer and of penance, of liturgy, study, and manual labor. It's physically hard, you wrote, but the compensation is interior peace.

This you have not found, or come close to finding. So the contract has been broken, the premise rendered invalid. Perhaps, as Mary Ruether suggested, it no longer makes sense for you.

Reading your letters, I sometimes think of the stories about longtime inmates who contrive to commit crimes so they'll be sent back to prison. They have lived by prison rules so long, they fear the freedom beyond the wall. You desperately want to get out but no longer believe you can endure life here in the world.

But you can.

Defect. Go with the woman you love, who says she loves you too. Have a child, perhaps. Do something about all that pain. There's no reason to endure such depression and anxiety alone; there's help of all sorts, from talking therapy to sophisticated medication.

Rejoin the world. Picket the White House. Write for The New Yorker. *Discuss the Sanctity of the Word on NPR. Hook up with Bill Moyers and really sell some books. Nobody will censor what you write or stop you from going anyplace on earth you want to see. You could even plunge into politics; your friends Dan and Phil Berrigan are still at it. Or you could publish those novels you've wanted to write. Find work you can do freely and joyously. Love God and live a full life, too.*

So go back to the gatehouse, thank the good brother who'd

been praying for you, and ask him to continue. Turn in your robes and your fifteenth-century Trappist underwear, take the train north to Manhattan and a cab right back to Columbia, whence you started out half a century ago.

I see you as a teacher. You once wrote that for a teacher to be absolutely sincere with generation after generation of students requires either supernatural simplicity or a kind of heroic humility. You possess both. You wrote a beautiful essay on the importance of mentors in your life. Be one. I'll be first in line.

And I'll help you get on-line. You'll need an introduction to the cyberculture to keep up with your students. We can E-mail each other.

I feel this way only because of what you yourself have written. Your way seems clear from your own lovely words and thoughts. Time for another kind of life of the spirit, the next journey of the soul.

Merton listened carefully, sipping another whiskey. He sat in silence for a long time, to be expected from a Trappist.

I couldn't keep still like a monk, so I went into the house, leaving Merton alone to think. I felt nervous about possibly upsetting him but good about being honest. That, to me, was what friendship was about.

Julius stayed with Merton, leaning his big head on Merton's lap for scratching. Stanley, whose spiritual life revolves around chasing balls and fetching sticks, followed me into the cabin. I made a pot of coffee.

An hour later I came outside to find Merton on his third whiskey. He'd have a cup of coffee, he said, glancing at the empty whiskey glasses, for safety's sake: he had a long drive home.

He thanked me for my hospitality and my frankness and expressed gratitude for the care with which I'd read and considered his work. He was always surprised, he told me, that anyone would read his writings. He glanced appreciatively at the big stack of his books on the picnic table.

Then he told me what I expected to hear. He understood what I was telling him and acknowledged that there was surely some truth in it. But he deeply loved God. He was committed to his life as a hermit, wedded to solitude; his bride was the silence. Imperfect as it was, Gethsemani was home. He didn't have the heart or health to build a whole new life. He'd made his decision, written about it, become famous all over the world for it.

Yes, he had doubts; yes, he was estranged from his religious order; yes, he needed love. But in the woods he felt joy, love, and mystery as well as loneliness and pain. For him, that would have to be enough.

Besides, there was a new abbot now. Merton was being censored less and was freer to travel. He was even considering bringing a phonograph to Mount Olivet so he could listen to music. Did I have any recommendations? And maybe the computer would be a good idea.

He clasped my hand, looked me in the eye. He told me to write. This time, he promised, he'd answer.

Soon he would vanish into the hermitage. Soon after that, he would die. This would be good-bye.

I took him into the cabin, where my PowerBook sat ready. I'd called up fifty Merton Web sites, including one maintained by the Merton Library outside Portland, Maine, where there was a Merton photo gallery.

He was astonished, transfixed. I also showed him a Web site run by his friend the Dalai Lama, then left him alone for half an hour or so.

From the kitchen, as I washed out the glasses, I heard childlike exclamations of delight and surprise as he clicked away. At least back in the hermitage he might be less lonely, with access to the world through the Net; his rich correspondence would likely deepen. He was, after all, the most interactive monk ever, in dialogue with countless people all over the world.

He hugged me, called me brother, blessed my small house. We knelt together, closed our eyes, and he said a prayer. Acknowledging our differences in religious belief, he had chosen a prayer, he said, that spoke to both of us. He translated from the Latin: "Let us always confess from our innermost breast, heart and strength that we are sinners and penitents, lest we be puffed up with pride at seeing some sign of piety in ourselves; but let us rather weep for our own and others' sins, because this is why we renounced the world and came to this place."

After he left, I felt a great sadness. My dogs circled anxiously, staying close. I wished that Merton really was here beside me so that I could talk to him for hours, commiserate about the authority figures plaguing us in both of our lives, and convince him that he was not failed and worthless but a great and loving man suffering from acute loneliness and other mysterious ailments out in the woods. I wished I had a prayer for him.

The emptiness and agony that marked the end of his life were frightening and dispiriting.

Perhaps it was arrogance to think Merton would ever come to me and that I would presume to know what to tell him. Or perhaps it was kinship.

Feeling my loneliness, I tried to fill myself up. I thought of Emma and the movies we'd soon catch up on. I thought of Paula and our twenty-fifth wedding anniversary looming in October and how we'd probably celebrate modestly, just the pair of us, at our local Thai restaurant. I thought of the on-line friends whose messages awaited me in my cabin, who wished me nothing but well.

I thought of my friend Jeff down in the valley, pictured him playing one day with his young children, and looked forward to the day when he and I could resume our leisurely walks in the woods with our dogs. It all helped.

IN 1968, JUST a few years into his hermitage and with a new abbot supervising Gethsemani, Merton was finally granted permission to accept a speaking invitation abroad, something denied for years despite his entreaties. He traveled to Asia, saw New Delhi, visited with the Dalai Lama in his mountain refuge. But he still couldn't resolve his ambivalence, telling friends he continued to feel "turbulence."

In December he was in Bangkok to lecture on Marxism and monastic perspectives, the reason for his trip. After the talk and lunch, he went to his room to rest. A delegate to the convention later wrote to Gethsemani to say that not long after Merton retired to his room, other people in his cottage heard a shout but thought they must have imagined it.

Merton was found dead in his room later that afternoon, on his back with an electric fan lying across his chest. The fan was still switched on, and there were a deep burn and some cuts on his right side and arm; the back of his head was bleeding slightly. The police concluded that he had somehow been electrocuted.

Merton's remains arrived at Gethsemani on December 17, 1968. Monks and friends chanted the funeral liturgy, and he was buried at dusk, under a light snowfall, in the monastic cemetery.

The real tragedy of Thomas Merton, it seemed to me, was that he made spirituality seem inaccessible even while exploring it so ceaselessly and courageously himself. If you weren't a monk, sacrificing yourself to God, working silently in the garden, falling to the floor to say psalms, how could you possibly be holy?

Such an experience lay beyond the grasp of many deeply spiritual people, who'd come to see the very word as reserved for someone else.

Merton wasn't obliged to be happy, and happiness wasn't, of course, the primary goal of life or spirituality; it was too transcendent and fragile an emotion. He defined the point of life as accepting faith and finding inner peace, purpose, and meaning. He seemed to have gotten no further than the first.

His dogmatic assertions that there was only one road to faith and fulfillment seemed to trap him. A man whose writings beautifully embodied the search for direction couldn't find one himself. A man who brought the idea of journeys of the soul to so many people suffered greatly on his own.

To Merton, solitude and holiness were linked. Solitude was the road to God. But up on my mountain, the Lonely One having departed, I was struck by the idea that he, more than anyone, was the author of his own loneliness.

When all was said and done, I wanted to have written a different story for myself.

Turning Toward the World

I am both a prisoner and an escaped prisoner.

—Thomas Merton, *Dancing in the Water of Life*

It was an odd sensation, leaving the house and not knowing when I'd be back. Clutching Lenny's "Last Resort" book, I went through the checklist for closing down the house.

Get everything away from the radiators.

Shut off the power to the electric stove and hot-water heater.

Turn off the switch in the bedroom that controlled the power to the TV and the VCR—which were not in the bedroom at all but in the living room; such were the charms of this place. Thieves could easily break in and take the equipment, but I'd be damned if they'd sprawl on the sofa and watch it here.

Stack firewood in a dry spot on the back porch. Clean out the fireplace, close the flue.

Set the thermostat to 45 degrees in every room where there were pipes.

Turn on the faucets, and let them run till the tank emptied. That way, if the power went out during subzero weather and the pipes froze, there wouldn't be enough water inside to burst them.

Take all perishable food out of the refrigerator and freezer. Put dog food, biscuits, and chew bones in cans. The mice, I knew, were just waiting for the sound of my van leaving the driveway.

Put mulch around the bushes and trees I'd planted, so they'd survive the winter. Pack up the begonias and take them home. Pull the storm windows down.

I expected to be back in a few weeks, to see the leaves turn and the mountainsides blaze, but I wasn't positive I could get away. One of the messages of Emma's surgery remained fresh in my mind—life is unpredictable. I had to shut the house down each time I left as if it were facing the dead of winter.

I didn't like leaving. As often as I thought the house was all set, I went back to check it again. I wasn't ready to turn back toward the world, not completely.

But summer was ending. All around, I could sense the season beginning to change. The sun was rising later, announced by fewer morning songbirds. The hummingbird I'd gotten to know had stopped coming to the feeder I kept filled with sugar water; she had been so stubbornly insistent on flying by regularly, checking to be sure it was stocked, that I guessed she had gone. The grass was turning brown; the nights were cooler; the light was changing.

Paula had been patient and uncomplaining, but I heard some weariness and loneliness in her voice when we spoke at night. Emma was getting sweet to me, always a sign that Dad had been away awhile. Friends were sending E-mail and leaving messages on my home answering machine wondering where I'd gone. I was falling behind on movies.

And Heidi had called to say it was time to organize the school car pool for the fall; how much driving would I be doing?

THIS QUESTION HAD more meaning than Heidi knew. There was nothing like a car pool to define one's life. Every morning the kids had to get to school, and every afternoon they had to come home; this was a sacrosanct task. Heidi's question was elemental. I felt poised on the cusp between two classic soul journeys, the adventure of parenthood and the challenges of whatever came next.

This would be my last year of car-pooling. By spring, Emma's friends would have driver's licenses. Em herself would have her learner's permit in a few months; in a blink, she'd be driving me. One of the great remaining tasks of modern parenthood would be completed.

When it came to driving, I had been one of the best, a champ, no small title in a state so overpopulated with cars and crisscrossed with highways. Tooling around New Jersey in a series of station wagons and minivans—a friend had nicknamed me the Prince of Rides—I racked up between fifteen and twenty thousand miles a year.

But the prince would soon fade into car-pool history and drive his last, retiring to tell tales of the time Lizzie threw up on the backseat, his heroic driving through the Great Storm of '94, and the Great Cream Cheese Fight of '96.

Down in the valley, Jeff and Michele were already beginning the great transition. Big men in trucks—some of the same ones I knew, in fact—were swarming all over their house, adding a bathroom, building a playroom. Emerging from shock to confront the reality of two infants arriving, Jeff and Michele were planning nurseries rather than gardens, fussing about nannies, taking out life insurance policies. It's a jarring moment in life when it's time for you to be the Grown-up.

My years as the Grown-up were winding down, however. Like Heidi, I was eager for this era to end. And like her, I dreaded the end as well, wondering how I would fill all the hours that would suddenly open up, how to prevent a gaping emotional void. Clearly, one way would be turning water pumps on and off, opening and closing up my house.

WHAT CAME TO my mind, as I ran through my checklist and started packing the van, wasn't the hawks circling or the glorious view but my daughter and something that had happened a couple of months earlier back in New Jersey. Left to their own, minds went where they wanted to.

We were at a riotously tacky carnival outside Giants Stadium in the Meadowlands. My time with Emma has, in many ways, been defined by a shared passion for tacky stuff: cheesy toys, amusement parks, video games, junk food, bad TV, stupid movies, seedy boardwalks.

This carnival was one of our high-water marks. We had just left the pig races. My daughter and her friend were on

the swing ride, where centrifugal force pushed the seats, sus-
pended by cables, higher and higher, flying farther out from
a central cylinder.

The carnival was so elaborately and brightly lit, in the vast
Meadowlands parking lot, that it looked beautiful, even
bounded by the headlights streaming past on Route 3. A different kind of beauty, I concede, from what I could see
upstate, but beauty all the same.

But in the distance, Manhattan's blaze let the carnival
know the difference between a painted lady and the real thing.

I waited below on the asphalt, next to a calzone stand,
staring up into the sky, transfixed by my daughter, her cop-
pery hair streaming out behind her, her feet sticking straight
into the air, laughing with her friend. I watched to see if she
still used her old trick of closing her eyes when the seats flew
high; she did.

I remembered her first ride, twelve years earlier in Wild-
wood, perhaps the only place tackier than the Meadowlands
Fair. My wife and I had strapped Emma into one of those tiny
wooden boats that circled a small tub of water. Then we
watched her ride slowly and gravely around and around as we
shouted encouragement, studied her face carefully for any
sign of terror or confusion, cheered her on. "Pull the bell,"
we yelled. "Pull the bell!" We made yanking gestures with our
hands and clapped when she found the rope and made the
little bell clang. What fools we must have seemed to the
bored teenagers who ran the rides.

And here I was all these years later, standing for perhaps
the last time beneath an amusement ride I had taken her to.
The following summer, if she still cared for such events, she

or one of her friends would be at the wheel, headed east on
Route 3. I would be tolerated at best, more likely prohibited.

It had gone by so fast, just as everyone always warned. It
was just a blink. Where would I be when I blinked again?
Where would she?

But I felt satisfaction as well as sorrow at the evolution of
that tiny person into the lovely young woman laughing high
above the concrete highways of New Jersey.

When my daughter was born, as I emerged from the
maternity unit, I swore that whatever had happened to my
family, whatever dumb mistakes I had made in life, all of that
would stay outside the room where my wife and daughter
were recovering together from the birth. It became an article
of faith. I would rewrite the sad history of my own family.

Now, watching Emma swing around and around, I told
myself that I had kept that promise. I had screwed up plenty
but had never really failed her. I had been loving, patient,
encouraging.

I had driven her tens of thousands of miles to camps, play
dates, drama classes, music lessons, rehearsals. I could not
begin to count the crises we had been through together: the
social cruelty of girls, the dramas about homesickness, the
previous summer's ordeal.

This was definitely faith for me: bringing a person into the
world, taking responsibility for her, doing as little harm as
possible and as much good. Making her laugh. Taking her to
the carnival every June. Telling her I loved her every day of
her life.

I had no way of knowing what ups and downs might follow that night in the Meadowlands. But I allowed myself a

moment of pride—not only in her, which is common, but in myself, which is rarer—as the ride began to slow and settle and I saw my daughter and her friend start to lower.

A pretzel vendor with a bronze Jersey Shore tan, lacquered dark hair, and a name tag—GERI—saw me watching and winked. "One of yours up there?"

"Yes," I said, pointing my daughter out.

"She looks like a nice kid from here," Geri said, generously, since she couldn't have seen much more than Emma's feet.

"She is," I said. And then blurted out, "You know what I was thinking? I must be a hell of a father to have helped raise a kid that great."

This cracked Geri up, and she laughed so contagiously that I joined in. We both understood the absurdity of the moment, its many subtexts.

Too bad that the nicest words I would ever hear about myself came from my own lips. But they were no less meaningful for that. And, as if to underscore my parenting, Geri gave me a pretzel for free, "for being a good dad." She said she wouldn't even think of taking $1.25.

TOWARD THE END of the summer, just before I closed the mountain house, Emma had come for a one-night look and made appropriately polite noises about how pretty the view was. I could almost hear her thinking, "What on earth am I supposed to do up here? What has this crazy man gone and done now?"

Watching her game struggles to be enthusiastic, I'd realized once again that this remained an ugly little cabin, with its odd furniture, dark paneling, and seventies carpeting. For weeks I'd been trying to convince us all that this would be a family vacation spot. Think of the skiing, I chirped. Or foliage season. Or picking fresh strawberries in the fields below. I was kidding all of us, and my daughter had seen through it.

"It's nice, Dad," she had said, patting me on the back and turning to study the Primestar program guide, which did impress her.

I squired her around the countryside for a day or so, but I could see her glancing at her watch as she murmured at the river and the farms.

We went to the county fair, where a recording of John Wayne narrating "America, the Beautiful" opened the rodeo and the rodeo master intoned a prayer in which he hoped our tickets were all paid in full when we got to heaven.

I had brought her to Mars, then foolishly presumed she would clap her hands for joy at the unfamiliar landscape. This had been my affair, not hers.

Now I felt oddly estranged, as if I'd been through something I couldn't explain, loved something for reasons that were not transferable.

Paula had understood this from the beginning. She'd come upstate for a weekend, liked the place enough, wondered how we were going to pay the mortgage, then stayed away while I encountered various ghosts, contemplated my life, and blazed away on my PowerBook. She could see the possibilities.

But the mountain was a less appealing place for a fifteen-year-old. And truth be told, we both grasped the underlying symbolism. On some level, I hadn't bought it as a place where I'd be responsible for a kid, but as a place where I wouldn't.

So the mountaintop was my place for now, on my head. There was no immediate reason for anybody but me to love it, though I hoped that my family would come to, over the next few years.

Disconnecting my computer, I felt like the plodding middle-class man in the movies who, confronted with the implications of his irresponsible and illicit choices, chickens out, breaks off the affair, leaves his lover behind.

This is the inevitable and moral choice. What kind of world would we live in if people didn't meet their responsibilities? What kind of husband and father and person would I be?

But I felt an almost physical pull, a grievous sense of loss, as if I were leaving a great love and feared never feeling such love again. The house was calling me back, bewildered as to why I was fleeing after it had served me so well. I was bereft, too. I was not quite old, no longer young; odds were I *had* experienced something I wouldn't feel again, at least not in the same way.

Like the guy in the movie, I felt an utter cliché, the wuss who chooses duty over passion. He returns to his responsibilities, but as he goes, he's looking over his shoulder regretfully. He knows he has to go back, but a part of him is screaming to run.

. . .

BUT YOU KNOW what? Affairs can be great tonics, especially this kind. They make us think and feel. They put our lives in context, force us to figure out what we love and what we don't.

For a few short-and-sweet weeks, I was gone from my usual world. I lived a spiritually rewarding life. I was recharged, if not reborn.

And then—who knows? This may even be the best part—I went home, to face the crises and try to solve the mysteries.

The house all closed up, the power and heat adjusted, I walked out onto the front lawn with Julius and Stanley. The Adirondack chair was stored in the shed; the picnic table on which I'd spread Merton's journals had been carted off by Lenny's family.

The faces and experiences of the summer crowded in on me as I sat on the grass. Nothing really extraordinary had happened, yet the summer felt overwhelming. The big men in trucks. The solitude. The well-diggers. The fires and storms. Lenny's death. Sitting by the Battenkill.

I remembered walking with Jeff, both of us enthralled and in shock at the idea of his onrushing double fatherhood. I remembered realizing those days were finally ending for me, and for good. I recalled our triumphal trip to the racetrack, our hikes in Vermont, my daily treks to Shushan.

It's so often hard to appreciate how happy you've been or how special an experience was until it's over. Packed up and ready to go, I began to grasp how much my time here had meant to me, how much I had learned.

Looking at this remarkably unremarkable little cabin, I saw clearly, and perhaps for the first time, just how grateful to it I was. How much I loved it. How well I intended to do by it. How much I planned to weave it into the history of my life and my family. Even in the summer sun, I began to plot how we'd spend Thanksgiving here, how we'd snowshoe and cross-country ski in the winter.

I felt whipsawed by different emotions. I had shed some scales. I wanted to stay. I needed to go. This was the best thing I'd ever done. It was the dumbest. I had come here to escape; I wanted very much to go home. I needed to prepare for the end of daily parenting. I wanted to take care of my kid.

Next to me, stuffed in bags for transport home, were all my Merton journals and books. I leafed through one volume until I found the description of his journey to Gethsemani. I read it several times, at first silently, then aloud.

> For I was now, at last, born: but I was still only new-born. I was living: I had an interior life, real, but feeble and precarious. And I was nursed and fed with spiritual milk. . . . For once, for the first time in my life, I had been, not days, not weeks, but months, a stranger to sin. And so much health was so new to me, that it might have been too much for me. And therefore I was being fed not only with the rational milk of every possible spiritual consolation, but it seemed that there was no benefit, no comfort, no innocent happiness, even of the material order, that could be denied me.

DARK TIMES

But this business of defeat is there, and I see it
is perhaps in some way permanent. . . . there
have been repeated failures, failures without
number, like holes appearing everywhere
in a worn-out garment.

—THOMAS MERTON, TURNING TOWARD THE WORLD

I'D THOUGHT A forest fire, a few thunderstorms, a bad well, and some loneliness meant I was growing humble. This was a monumental conceit, a shallow perception of my own experience that cried out for—and received—a whupping.

I'd had the gall to believe that I was putting some of life's trials and dramas—parenting, work crises, financial insecurity—behind me. Within a few weeks I expected to sign contracts for several books, along with various magazine articles and other projects.

I figured I was about to make more money than I had ever earned, as a writer or anything else. At last we could start paying down our pile of debt, saving more money for retirement and Emma's college tuition, ridding the mountain house of its remaining eyesores and beginning the long, tedious, and expensive process of renovating our house in New Jersey—so leaky, peeling, and neglected that we'd been too embarrassed to invite friends for dinner for several years.

None of these were unrealistic expectations. It was no longer a question of whether I could make it as a writer; I *had* made it.

Instead, those legendary and devilish fates were just chuckling, waiting for me to descend from my lofty perch so they could smack me around.

By January, the dark time upstate, most of my writing projects were gone. Much of the income I was counting on had vanished with them, along with the confidence, peacefulness, and spiritual nourishment of the summer.

And the little house on the mountain had never seemed a more foolish idea.

I'D DRIVEN UP a few times earlier in the winter, and the weather had been uncharacteristically benign. In the crisp sunlight, the mountain was beautiful, the light clear, the surrounding hills radiant.

I had many sweet moments. At night, when my work was done, the supper dishes washed, fresh firewood brought in from the porch, the dogs walked, after Emma and Paula had reported in, safe at home, I lit a fire, sipped from a glass of Drambuie or Glenlivet, read a novel.

Taken in small doses, as a counterpoint to a frantic urban life, the quiet was delicious, even healing, the cozy and bright cabin an island of warmth and light in a forbidding void. I had to give Lenny and his father credit: the house was snug even on bitter winter days. The brick fireplace took up nearly an entire wall; after a blaze had been burning for an hour or two, the brick itself warmed and could heat the house almost by itself.

Reading in a recliner, listening to the logs pop, I thought this might be as peaceful as life had ever been for me, or would ever get.

But the warm, sweet moments were just that—moments: the exception, not the rule. Winter days were usually harsh and lonely, the antithesis of the way I'd always imagined human beings were meant to live.

By January, spending a couple of weeks here with the dogs, I had no trouble picturing some depressed or frightened person walking out onto a mountain overlook like this one in the dead of winter, taking a seat in an Adirondack chair, and going to sleep for good. How could Merton, alone for weeks in his primitive cabin with far fewer amenities and much less human contact than I had, feel anything but despair?

On a night when the wind was shrieking through the trees, it seemed as if every warm, happy, or living thing was gone, sucked away by the cold and wind.

In the summer the mountaintop had teemed with life— birds, deer, chipmunks, frogs, squirrels, raccoons, all those bugs—and with light. The sun had blazed across the valley at dawn and hung around until long after dinner.

Now only my old nemeses, the mice, were afoot, still scampering in the basement, still battling me for the house. I heard them skittering around the kitchen at night. In fact, I was still catching one or two a day in my traps.

I contemplated a truce, tossing out the peanut butter, letting bygones be bygones. Experiencing winter, I had keener empathy for their determination to get inside and stay there. Maybe it was time to share. At least the mice were warm-blooded and alive, and I wanted all the company I could get.

Across the valley, the pale sky seemed to melt into the snow-covered hills until I couldn't tell one side of the horizon from the other. Most of the time, a shroud of mist produced indistinguishable shades of gray. The mountain I'd gazed at, which popped up grandly, sometimes spectacularly, nearly every summer morning, had not been visible all week. I missed it.

BUYING MY HOUSE on the mountain had been an affirmation of my future as a writer. It was the place where I intended to do my best work, find the privacy I deserved, get the space I needed to think. Writing made it necessary for me to run to the mountain, made me feel entitled to it. And my writing would pay for it.

But just a couple of weeks after I'd closed up the mountain house at summer's end, everything seemed different, worse.

My publisher abruptly canceled my mystery series, and more than half of my income along with it. Along with the mysteries, a novel I had planned to write on the mountain next summer was summarily rejected by half a dozen publishers. It wasn't me, my agent said soothingly. She was hearing the same story all day long. Publishing was in crisis, going through one of those contractions that American businesses regularly suffer.

It also turned out that the nonfiction book I was writing on the mountain needed considerable work. Which meant there wouldn't be a second nonfiction book to write for a long time, or even the final payment for the first. Meanwhile, a recent paper edition of my first novel had sold so poorly that

I received a fax announcing that it was no longer worth warehousing and would shortly be shredded. My financial plans and expectations were collapsing like a house made of Popsicle sticks.

Everybody told me not to take these suddenly hard times personally. Writers go through this, people reminded me; there are ups and downs, cycles and twists.

Paula assured me the tide would turn. Jeff said I was being too dramatic. My agent said others had it much worse; I was lucky to have my nonfiction book contract and my "Hotwired" columns. But I don't believe praise, only criticism; I can never accept reassurance.

Just a few months earlier, I'd bought the house with the idea of writing there very much in mind. Now I feared that my life as a writer might be over.

I COULDN'T HAVE conjured up a more fitting place and time to retreat, to lick my wounds and brood. The mountain was lost in snow and fog. It was gloomy morning and evening; I hadn't seen sunlight in three days. Night arrived in the late afternoon.

Stanley and Julius had crawled into bed with me at 3:00 A.M. our first night here and every night since. Neither would budge. With Stanley's head on my shoulder, Julius's on my arm, we were four hundred or so pounds of dog and owner in a furry heap at the top of the world, trying to stay warm and provide mutual comfort.

They went to sleep, but I couldn't. Fear kept me up, as it had much of the fall. Soon, in an incongruous scene, both dogs were snoring as I stared at the ceiling wondering if I'd survive or be able to pay my bills, certain to grow exponentially as names like Brown, Wesleyan, and Yale were being mentioned with increasing frequency in my other house.

The question that kept me wide awake was, How many comebacks does somebody like me get? I'd already had quite a few. But the new reality was that I was fifty. There might not be time for many more.

In the darkness, I waited for some answer. I had hung Merton's picture on my office wall, had brought the usual stack of his books up with me. But Merton was quiet. At my age, he had felt defeated, utterly and finally. No holy man was going to appear on the mountain to tell me what to do.

I told myself this: there is no cap on comebacks. One can't hide behind age, especially mine. That was the cheapest kind of excuse.

At some point, I realized, I had to look inward, not outward. Publishers, readers, agents, critics could make my life easier or harder, richer or poorer, but they couldn't ultimately determine what I should be doing or how well I could do it.

I couldn't allow others to define me. I couldn't hide behind middle age. I couldn't blame the vagaries of publishing. I couldn't even blame the crisis in "mid-list" publishing that was, I was reading, decimating writers like a cultural scourge.

What I could do—actually, *all* I could do—was have faith in me. And do better work. Out of trouble, yet another opportunity. Out of solitude, time to think. Out of reflection, a sense of what to do.

Perhaps I could accomplish something here that I had not been able to do in nearly a half-century—to believe that I had a worthwhile place to be in the world, important things to contribute; to accept that I, more than anyone or anything else, could guide the way I fared.

To even begin to believe this was momentous. It suggested a life with less fear and more freedom, an exhilarating kickoff to life after fifty, a monumental birthday present to myself.

I couldn't give up on me.

INSTINCTIVELY, I'D DRAWN up some psychic survival rules for the winter, seeing right away that I would have to fight the loneliness and the cold head-on, or it would consume me. I took the dogs on two or three walks, no matter the weather, and threw the ball for Stanley, even though the ground was so hard the ball sometimes skidded halfway down the mountain before he caught up.

I drove out on at least one excursion a day, sometimes to Yushak's Market, sometimes to the dump, sometimes to consult Steve at the hardware store. I called friends after dinner to chat for a few minutes.

It was critical to set up a routine and keep it. Get up early, go to sleep early, spend less time in the dark. I feared losing discipline, cutting corners.

Chastened by wanderings in the woods and numerous other mishaps of the summer, I took the elements seriously. In the cold I wore a thermal undershirt, thick socks, heavy waterproofed hiking boots. I had a Polartec fleece pullover, a winter storm coat, a nerdy hat with earflaps and a visor, gloves meant for below-zero temperatures. I pulled most of them on even if I was just walking to get firewood. I kept the cell phone charged and carried it with me like a talisman.

On one nighttime excursion outside for wood, the door of the house blew shut and locked behind me. I had a spare key hidden nearby, luckily, but by the time I found it and staggered back to the house with the wood, the wind had sucked nearly every bit of warmth from my body. I sat shivering for half an hour.

Three times I'd fallen on the ice, once banging my head. It didn't take much imagination to picture lying there for several hours until, eventually, Jeff or some sheriff's deputy came looking for me and found me a block of ice. I put notes in my wallet and glove compartment listing Jeff's phone number and my mountain and Jersey addresses, in case the car slid into a telephone pole or I fell hard and lost consciousness. "There are two yellow Labs back in the house," I wrote on the note. "Their names are Julius and Stanley. They are friendly."

On cold mornings, I warmed up the car to make sure the battery stayed charged. I was careful to keep enough food on hand for a few days, should a sudden storm hit. I'd heard plenty of horror stories about sudden savage blasts of snow and ice whooshing down from Canada, dumping three, even four feet of snow with little warning. I kept dry firewood stacked on the porch, enough for a few days if the power went out.

Meanwhile, as I worked to stay warm, safe, and productive, while fearing the collapse of my writing career and the loss of my upstate aerie, it was getting close to the twins' birth. Jeff and Michele were rushing off to doctors, scrambling to buy car seats and changing tables. The twins had names now: the boy would be Milo, the girl Georgia. I was already making plans for Disney World. I'd taken Emma when she was barely eighteen months and she remembered nothing about it. Maybe I'd take the twins when they were three or four.

Jeff and I spoke often, but he was increasingly entering the state of distraction and panic I remembered well, even with one baby. Having children broadened people in the long run, but new babies could shrink their lives pretty dramatically for a while.

I'd agreed to be the twins' legal guardian, pleased to be asked but sobered at the thought of acquiring two babies and the wolfish Lulu. The Prince of Rides would never emerge from his van. I prayed for long life and health for these new parents.

One night when the fog lifted, I badgered Jeff to see the movie *Titanic* with me, thinking it might be some time before he saw another. On the drive to Bennington, he understood what I had hoped to be more subtle about.

"You scared me when you pushed me to go see this movie tonight. You don't think I'll get to the movies for years, do you?"

No, no, I said. I just wanted you to see it on the big screen, not wind up renting a video.

Sure, he said, smiling. He knew.

Not years, I said. Months, maybe even eight or nine months, but not years.

He loved the movie.

. . .

IT WAS THE fifth day of gloom, this time with rain teeming from the sky and sluicing down the roads and hills. An enormous cloud sailed right over the house and sealed it off, a white wall. I had the spooky sensation of flying, in a house disconnected from the earth.

I wasn't going to send any more novel proposals to be rejected, I had decided over the past few dark days. There was a message here, and I was beginning to understand that it had little to do with age, fate, or the economics of publishing. My ideas hadn't been good enough, nor my writing strong enough. I needed to wait, to come up with better ones. Though it's more satisfying to blame other people for your troubles, the problem is that it ultimately doesn't help you get what you want. Eventually, with some patience—and yes, some faith—I would come up with the right idea for a novel. And I'd sell it. Some writers would survive this panic; I intended to be one of them.

Meanwhile, it was time to stop hopscotching across several venues and start doing a better job in one or two. As long as I could afford it, I'd concentrate on my nonfiction work and my Web writing.

This made sense but didn't wash away the fear. The whole predicate on which I had changed my life—becoming a writer, making a living at it—seemed shaky now, the house on the mountain indefensible, pure indulgence and denial.

To make matters worse, I had commissioned a new screened front porch for the mountain house, and a cleared meadow. The last of the summer's men in trucks, Loren and

Wes, had come up in the fall, knocked away the old porch and an ugly concrete patio, and begun building a beautiful new screened enclosure with a gabled roof and electrical outlets for my laptop. I could read and write, eat, and just stare in this spectacular setting, shaded from the sun and freed from bugs.

Then Loren rode up in a giant bulldozer and began clearing almost two acres of saplings, brush, and organic debris that had accumulated on the slope below the house, obscuring so much of the view that neighbors warned me there wouldn't be any left in a few more years.

The work, undertaken in the belief that I'd have more than enough money to pay for it, was too far along to stop when the cancellations and rejections began to pile up. Trucks were back on the mountain, along with stacks of plywood and cinder blocks. Not only would we be unable to pay off our debts, I had just added more bills.

In January the new meadow was covered in snow and ice, but my view was twice as open and beautiful. I couldn't wait for spring, when I could sit on the porch with my coffee and read and write all day. That is, if I still had the house.

I knew the right thing to do. Twice I called Georgette and left messages on her answering machine. Had she called back, I meant to tell her to put the cabin up for sale; I couldn't afford two houses now. But Georgette was off on vacation and didn't call back. The locals knew when to get away.

I thought Paula would be delighted when I told her the plan; instead she was annoyed. "That's an impulsive, unthinking response," she said. "You can't just quit like that. Don't just decide on your own to get rid of it. Let's see what happens." Our usual yin and yang. Even when nothing would have made her happier than having the house off our hands, she remained steady and cautious.

On the sixth day of my deep-winter stay, the mountain across the valley finally popped out of the mist, along with the half-dozen or so smaller mountains alongside. It was mesmerizing to watch the layers of clouds and fog peel off and the valley reveal itself slowly but steadily, hill by hill, farm by farm. I thought I could see the dairy cows I looked for each morning when they strolled out of their barn and into the distant field.

SITTING IN HIS lonely hermitage in the woods, brooding and fuming about his life as a monk, Merton recorded the remarkable moment when he asked himself, late in life, as elemental a question as anyone can pose: "Who am I?"

His answer was forthright, instinctive: "A son of God."

Sitting on my mountain in the dead of winter at an unexpectedly bleak moment in life, I found myself asking the same question. But I had no ready answer.

People who take risks and win are visionaries, prescient heroes; people who gamble and lose are just fools. I was tilting toward the second. But like the monk said, if you want to be in the Book of Life, you have to live. That was the judgment I'd have to risk, well aware that the line between one category and the other was sometimes so narrow as to be invisible.

Life without dreams is the absence of hope. In a sense, dreams *are* faith, especially for people like me. Dreams sustain and propel us.

Coming to the mountain for this bleak stretch of bitter cold, fog, snow, and rain, in what had been a grim and wounding season, was a powerful experience. I'd come nose to nose with a dream lost, and one—this lovely place—at least partially fulfilled.

So part of the challenge for me up here was to find the time and space to forge some new dreams. This, I found, couldn't be done instantly, any more than real contemplation or meditation can. It takes time, space, patience, solitude, work, and opportunity.

I had gone to considerable trouble and expense to find all of these. What did I have to show for it?

Those kinds of expectations, I knew instinctively, were dangerous. You can't will yourself to instantly forge exciting new directions for yourself any more than you can command yourself to believe in God; to try is to invite defeat and disappointment. You have to give change the chance to happen.

What was clear was that the landmark passages of life— having kids, sending them off to college, turning fifty—had to be honored, in my case, by seizing the opportunity to find fresh dreams and set off in pursuit of them.

And over time I found a few:

I dreamed of making the transition from hovering dad to supportive friend and father. I wanted to support Emma in whatever she chose to do, rather than make choices for her. I wanted her to take my support and affirmation absolutely for granted.

I dreamed of renewing my marriage, although this had nothing to do with vows or receptions, but with brutal candor and clear visions. As Paula and I headed into middle age, I saw that she felt increasingly vulnerable, as did I. We got tired earlier, had less reserve, saw a bit less clearly, heard a tad less distinctly. We didn't feel old—we weren't yet—but we could begin to see what growing old would feel like.

And that was yet another dream: to age well. Many of my friends had banished the subject of aging or tried to deny it in other ways. I hardly knew a woman Paula's age who didn't dye her hair, and I frequently saw men joining them. Friends jogged, ran, pumped feverishly, even excessively, as if they could fend off time.

I didn't want to deny age. I wanted to see it clearly and, insofar as was possible, make the most of it.

In childhood and in current life, I'd seen how much difficulty and resentment aging generated in couples. I saw how hard it was for a spouse to no longer be heard, to absorb the growing list of things that could no longer be done or at least not done the same way. I'd noticed how short-tempered and frustrated partners could get with each other, as if—like the maniacally exercising men—they were willing the people they loved to stay young.

I dreamed of never resenting Paula for growing older, of never diminishing her or making her feel incompetent about things she couldn't control. If I struggled to have faith in myself, I'd never have to encourage her to have faith in me. Aside from loving her, I owed her, and I dreamed that I would be an honorable and loving old man who paid his debts. I hoped the people around us would see not a grumpy couple exasperated with each other but a loving pair strolling together toward the end of their lives. A couple Emma wouldn't mind being around.

When I died, I told Emma, I wanted to be cremated. I wanted it understood that anyone who shed a tear would be tossed from whatever service might be held, and that whoever remained had to tell a funny story about what a strange, exasperating person I was. I wanted the laughter and hooting to be heard a hundred yards away, preferably accompanied by Van Morrison or Aretha.

Meanwhile, another dream: I wanted to move from one good work to another, sort of a Goodwill Johnny Appleseed. I could help Jeff brace for parenting, help another friend through the grief of new widowhood. Then maybe I'd tutor a faltering kid in English. As I moved from one task to the next, I'd pick up friends and satisfactions along the way, so that at my memorial service all sorts of people would pop up to surprise Emma and Paula with stories of how helpful and generous I'd been.

I wanted to remain a writer and become a better and more successful one. I couldn't wait for my comeback. I wanted to write till I dropped, to be found slumped over a Macintosh keyboard.

There were plenty of other dreams bubbling in these short, solitary days. I was still mulling them over, wondering which were worth chasing. Dreams needed to weather and age.

But those I was sure about constituted a pretty good start. They felt solid, worthwhile, doable, likely to pass the test of time.

YOU COULDN'T REALLY plan for the Perfect Day. You were in it before you even knew it was a possibility. It required a complicated convergence; a dozen forces—weather, stars, friends, family, work, chemistry, mood—had to operate in perfect harmony. But when it happened, it was a wonder—a no-hitter, a best-seller, nirvana.

Perfect Days are fragile. A sick kid could undo one; so could an unhappy spouse. Or money troubles, bad news from an agent, a backache.

And there were other obstacles. My family was not here. When perfect things befell me, I wanted Paula and Emma to be around to share them.

I could remember one Perfect Day the three of us had had at the Bronx Zoo when Emma was little, and another on the vast, rolling dunes outside Provincetown. We all communed with the spirits of Eugene O'Neill, Edward Hopper, and the other creators who lived and worked there, and we left them small gifts—poems, pencils, toys—in the sand.

But over time, since I'd bought this house, I'd learned that if I knew Paula and Emma were busy and happy, a Perfect Day was at least possible. I was learning to let them go, for a few days at a time. This was good for them and for me, essential practice for a highly involved dad whose pride and joy was already poring through college catalogues.

I had resolved not to be one of those whining boomer parents, left shell-shocked and empty by the departure of their children. Wasn't that our job, to make ourselves dispensable? I wanted to celebrate Emma's independence, not mourn it.

A walk with Jeff and our dogs through some idyllic landscape could make for a Perfect Day, but the twins' impending birth was bearing down on him like a bullet train. He was rushing to finish his book, paint the nursery, stock his new freezer.

We caught a cup of coffee now and then, talked constantly on the phone, stayed very much in touch. Our friendship had adapted, evolved, held its ground. But it wasn't, couldn't be, the same.

Julius and Stanley were always there, happily for me. Their lives were uncomplicated. Whenever I was ready to go out, they were, too. Wherever I wanted to go was fine with them. We had shared this journey and were now inseparable.

And later in January, as the dark times were beginning to yield, the light starting gradually to return, we three had a Perfect Day together. I'd driven up to bring Jeff and Michele a load of groceries—the sort of take-out goodies, from sourdough bread to exotic greens, it was hard to find in Yokumville—and to attend a baby shower some friends were throwing. It was a short visit, two or three days, no more.

I arrived at their house in late afternoon, stashed calf's liver and soup in the freezer. Michele, increasingly immobile, looked exhausted. The house was in disarray from the last-minute improvements under way. Lumber was stacked everywhere. Piles of dishes sat in the kitchen sink. I could see Jeff and Michele's exquisite aesthetic sensibilities giving way to the reality of kids, even before they were born. Everything would, I knew, get a lot messier.

Jeff and I did the dishes together as Michele went upstairs to rest. Then, before I could quite register its arrival, a Perfect Day began.

8:00 P.M. JEFF and I made some tea and sat down in his darkened living room—soon to be known, I predict, as the family room—with a fire crackling in the old fireplace. Lulu, Julius, and Stanley, siblings now in a way, piled in a heap by the hearth, at ease and asleep.

We launched into a marathon bullshit session about what it meant to be a man and a father.

I talked about the strange rituals of fatherhood—diaper changing, feeding, pushing the stroller—and the difficulty men sometimes had in getting and staying close to their children, as well as their friends. People often looked at me strangely, wondering what I was doing hanging around schools and supermarkets in the middle of the day. It was supposedly the era of the Sensitive Involved Father, but there weren't all that many in evidence.

I warned Jeff that being one could be more of a struggle than he imagined—teachers, doctors, neighbors, and friends often didn't expect men to be involved in the intimate details of their children's lives. It would be so easy to leave the details of child care to women. But if you did, bit by bit, you could lose touch with the minutiae of your children's lives: who their friends were, what the pediatrician was like, what favorite toys had to be tucked in with them at night.

Jeff recalled a different set of rituals from his own family—camping, hunting, and building. He felt so sorry, he said, that all the men in his family—his father, grandfather, and brother, men who had been so important to him—were dead and that Milo and Georgia would never know them. Like mine, Jeff's family had been shattered. His parents had divorced when he was a teenager; his father had died of lung cancer, his brother of AIDS.

We talked about our fathers and the difficult and unhappy lives they had had, how I had struggled valiantly to do better by my kid than my father had done by us. Jeff was as determined to forge a new history for his family.

Being a man was more complicated for us, we agreed. Unlike women, we had no real movement, with all the attendant magazines, support groups, and sense of community, and few role models.

We talked about how hard it was for men to make friends, and how determined we each were that our friendship survive the intense changes bearing down on both of our lives. Then we whined about how difficult writing was.

Women take such conversations for granted, but for men, they are rare, precious. And poignant, too, at least for me. I wasn't being completely honest. Deep down, I doubted that our friendship could survive all these changes intact, or that we'd ever have many more conversations like this one. Our talk was rich, funny, open, high-quality bullshit in a safe place with a great friend. Three hours passed by in a flash, until Michele descended to order me out. Her back was hurting. "I need my husband," she announced.

11:00 P.M. THE dogs and I headed up to the mountain. A nearly full moon lit up the valley and turned the snowy mountaintop to glistening silver. I went through my settling-in ritual—turning on the water pump, the heat, the hot-water heater. I heard the pump hum and the pleasing sound of water splashing into the tank and the pipes.

Though it was late, it was too beautiful not to go outside. We took a walk through the woods, along the very route where I had gotten lost in July. Now I knew it as well as my block back home, even in midwinter at midnight. We walked in complete silence for nearly half an hour, my boots crunching on hard snow the only sound.

To bed. My bedroom—which used to be the study—was dark and restful, the mountain utterly still, my new bed warm and comfortable. I slept well, longer and more deeply than I had in years.

6:30 A.M. IT was a two-dog night. I booted Julius and Stanley out of bed, showered, made some coffee. It was a day of cold but brilliant sunshine. Outside for our morning walk, I found the air piercing; it hurt my lungs, and made my toes and fingers ache. A small cloud had snagged on the big mountain across the valley. Around it, snowy peaks in shadowy hues turned brown, blue, and purple, as the sun moved in and out of the clouds.

The snow was hard enough to give Stanley's rubber ball the necessary bounce. I tossed it down the slope of my new meadow-to-be a good twenty times as Stanley vaulted over hillocks, plowed through snowdrifts, and crashed through the underbrush in dogged pursuit. Julius sat next to me and sighed.

7:30 A.M. I called Paula, who was headed to the city on a story. Emma would go directly from school to her job at a funky local bookstore. Both were fine.

Settling in my study, turning on my PowerBook, I looked up at the poster of Merton and received his smile, my daily benediction. It was a warm portrait, one that captured the spirit of the man, and I always started writing with a nod to it. He, of all people, understood precisely what I was doing and why. He approved, I knew it. He was encouraging me, egging me on, watching with pleasure as I struggled to find faith in myself.

To warm up, to feel inspired but not pretentious, I read a bit at random from Merton's journals and Mencken's essays.

Reading Mencken and Merton together was one of my better moves up here, each complementing the other. I couldn't help fantasizing about a Merton-Mencken talk show on cable, a vastly improved version of *Crossfire*.

Merton was forever challenging me to be brave, to keep searching. Mencken kept my feet on the ground, reminding me constantly and sometimes brutally to be humble, to stay honest, to beware of sentimentality and pomposity. When I drifted too far afield, I considered with a shudder what he might say if he were around to read what I wrote.

8:30 A.M. I started writing and didn't stop for four hours. For no reason I could ever isolate or analyze, sometimes prose just flowed, a pure steady stream. This was one of those too-rare times. I felt refreshed by it, not tired but energized, not ready to rest but eager to keep working. Every hour or so, I scuttled to the kitchen to make myself some tea, then hustled back to the computer.

. . .

12:30 P.M. I made myself a tuna sandwich and ate quietly, looking out the kitchen window, thinking about nothing in particular. The light and view were lifting me up, though, raising my spirits. It was almost as if a person who had such loveliness to look at would find a way to rise to the setting, one way or another.

1:00 P.M. THE dogs and I headed off for Vermont. I had a vague idea of visiting the bookstore in Manchester; I was out of novels and had plans for the night. I'd brought in a big stack of firewood and dusted off the Glenlivet, but I lacked an essential, a good book.

Fifteen miles from my mountain, I passed something called the Merck Forest, which I must have driven by a dozen times over the summer and never noticed. Turning off the state highway, I followed a snowy road for half a mile until I came to a parking area.

Near the parking area was the start of the Discovery Trail. Except for footprints, the path was empty, windswept and starkly beautiful. The snow on either side was dazzling, the purest white I'd ever seen.

I'd forgotten to take my phone. Back home, people make fun of me when I tell them that upstate in winter I carry a cell phone everywhere, but a day or two on my mountain when light and heat vanished at 3:00 P.M. would explain in a hurry. If I fell or got lost in this forest, it wouldn't be like stumbling about in the woods behind my house in midsummer.

But I had brought a fresh thermos of tea, which emboldened me and my dogs to set off on a trail that looked, from the map mounted on a wooden board, to be about five miles long.

It started off downhill, then wound through the woods and started climbing. Every so often we came to a wooden bench, where I stopped to drink some tea and look out at snowy trees and misty mountains. We encountered no one, heard nothing. All was beauty and peacefulness. The very process of thinking was different in a place like this, purer, clearer.

Stanley was as happy as I'd ever seen him, bounding through the woods, finding choice branches to bring me, barking in pure joy. Eventually, he even got Julius excited, and the two of them tore off into the trees. Every fifty yards or so both would stop abruptly, turn, and look at me. Is this much fun okay? they seemed to be asking. Then they'd take off again, surprised by their own freedom.

After an hour my feet and fingers grew stiff. I wasn't really properly dressed for a long hike. And as the sun began to descend, the cold took on a different, more menacing quality. It was time to head back.

The bulletin board in the parking lot explained that this preserve was community-owned and -run. I decided to join up. There were classes that might teach me about nature, that still elusive force I was learning to live with but didn't truly understand, and the Forest needed volunteers to help keep the place operating. I'd be back.

Back in the car, Julius and Stanley fell instantly asleep. But despite our trek in the snow, I wasn't really tired. I realized, belatedly, that this was probably the most beautiful walk I'd ever taken, anywhere. And that it would take Thoreau, not me, to do it justice.

3:00 P.M. IN Manchester I visited the Northshire Bookstore, where I'd been a steady customer and was—every time—instantly recognized and welcomed as an author by the book-savvy staff. It was pleasant to be reminded of that. I bought two novels. Up here, having good books to read is as vital as heat. Tonight, I had the perfect end to this emerging Perfect Day all mapped out.

4:30 P.M. THE boys and I swept into the haunted town of Shushan, my nearest downtown, an oddly atmospheric hamlet on the way to nowhere.

Half the buildings at its central crossroads are for rent. There's a strange museum filled with medieval European art, and a covered bridge. Not far from Janet's Beauty Salon and Yushak's Market stands the brick headquarters of the Shushan Volunteer Brigade, the very heroes who would have rushed up the mountain to save my house, or at least hose down its remains, after a forest fire.

I'd met the Shushan potter, whose name was Bill Burrell, and his half-domesticated dog, Abbie, the first week I came upstate. He'd endeared himself to me forever: a young artist struggling to make a living in a remote place, he'd nevertheless rushed out and bought several of my books.

Abbie, whom Bill had found lying in the road and taken in, was the Queen of Shushan, strolling back and forth across the street at will, visiting friends in the stores, cadging treats, running off strays. All summer, whenever I drove into town to pick up the newspaper or buy groceries at Yushak's, I'd left a dog biscuit for her on Billy's stoop. By now she knew my car a block away and came flying.

This day, as I pulled into town, Billy ran out from his storefront to give me a bear hug. We sat in his shop to catch up. He wanted to teach me to throw a pot. I liked the idea and offered to bring lunch. We jawed about the loneliness of upstate winters; he and his girlfriend had broken up a couple of years before. Loneliness draws people together here, binds them like any shared ordeal. Everyone has his own way of dealing with it and passes along tips and insights to others.

"You have to go out, and keep going out," Billy advised. "You can't give in to the cold and the dark."

I told him that when I next came back—when the twins were born, most likely—we would get together. I wanted to learn a bit of his craft, to make something myself for my house.

5:00 P.M. I had the virtuous tiredness that comes when you've done something demanding but healthy and feel entitled to rest. It was nearly dark as I pulled into my driveway.

Jeff had left a message, to make sure I wasn't freezing in a snowdrift somewhere (Emma had charged him with keeping me alive). I called back to yak. "I've had a Perfect Day," I told him, like a proud kid reporting to his dad. "It was gorgeous on the mountain. I wrote two neat chapters, and I went for the most beautiful hike of my life and visited in Shushan. And now I've got two novels to read."

After dinner I washed the dishes, vacuumed, took my exhausted dogs for a final stroll, built and lit a fire. As the flames caught, I checked in at home, happily reporting to Paula that I'd had one of the best days of my life, advising Emma on some minor adolescent crisis.

Soon, the fire roaring, I started reading one of my new novels, sipping every now and then from a glass of my shrinking supply of Scotch.

MIDNIGHT: STUNNED TO glance at my watch, I looked out the window and saw the snow lit up by the moon. I walked out onto the porch to stare.

I'd worked and walked, thought and yakked, talked to my wife, counseled my kid, chatted with my close friend. I'd seen beautiful vistas. I felt peaceful and happy.

I had no idea when to expect the next Perfect Day. It might be months or years away. The days in between might be decidedly imperfect and bumpy. But I was delighted, blessed, to have had this one, at this time, in this place.

EPILOGUE

*Inexorably, life moves on towards crisis and
mystery. . . . In a way, each one judges himself
merely by what he does. Does, not says. Yet let us
not completely dismiss words. They do have meaning. They are related to action. They spring from
action and they prepare for it, they clarify it,
they direct it.*

—THOMAS MERTON, TURNING TOWARD THE WORLD

THERE WAS NO longer much ugliness to be seen outside my little house on the mountain. The cinder blocks circling the big maple—Lenny's decorations—had been filled in
with topsoil; flowers and vines obscured the gray concrete. A
rock garden was already sprouting where the old polluted well
had been.

The benches, debris, and odd signs out back had been
carted away by Tim or buried by Loren's bulldozer, all traces
of them now gone. So were the slime-filled plastic swimming
pool and the craters marking the search for the septic tank.

The vast forest of tall weeds, raggedy saplings, and
untamed bushes that had threatened to obscure the view and
helped shroud the house in bugs and dust had been bull-
dozed magically away. Gone too were the ugly shrubs and
crumbling concrete patio.

If I hadn't taken snapshots before closing, I'd hardly have been able to recognize the forlorn property I first looked at in what I saw now. Last summer seemed much further than a few months away. So did the bitter bleakness of winter.

The apple trees I'd planted had taken root and were beginning to blossom; the scrawny red maple had survived the winter to bud and leaf, and so had the butterfly bushes by the rear corner of the house. Scores of tulips were sprouting, and the begonia I'd nurtured all winter back in New Jersey was restored to its spot by the side door.

In a couple of weeks I'd hang out the hummingbird feeder and drag out the Gothic birdbaths I'd bought and stored in the basement. I had become enchanted by birdsong, my alarm clock and private chorale, my ode to joy.

It was late April, and the dogs and I had returned to the mountaintop for a springtime visit. I wanted to dewinterize the house, turn off the heat, turn on the water, put up the screens, survey my handiwork, and experience the one season I had yet to encounter on the mountain.

A lot had changed.

Milo and Georgia had arrived in mid-March, after a healthy, natural birth. The nanny was competent and affectionate, the freezer was full, the microwave useful, Jeff and Michele gaunt and exhausted but happy. I met the newcomers when they were two days old, treasured holding them and reading them stories they were years too young to comprehend. I told Georgia about my time in television (she was fascinated) and complained to a sympathetic Milo about my publishers. I loved watching them sleep—and then handing them back to their rest-deprived parents and driving up to the peace of my own solitary cabin.

Although Jeff and I checked in by phone for a few minutes every few days, our firelit bull session on the Perfect Day was the last long talk we'd had.

Meanwhile, my new, two-acre meadow was sprouting with yellowish-green stalks—the forerunners of grasses and wildflowers—that lit up the mountainside, highlighted the valley below, and would soon rustle sweetly in the breeze.

My gabled and screened porch, spacious and grand, opened for business. It jutted proudly out over the mountaintop, taking full advantage of the even-more-spectacular view the cleared meadow had created. Once I assembled the table and chairs waiting in the shed, I'd have the writing spot and refuge I'd dreamed of for more than a decade—for a lifetime, really. I'd never have nightmares about dying up here. In fact, I'd be proud to keel over onto my PowerBook, facing the mountains. This porch was now my favorite single spot in the world.

But no resting on laurels. Later in the spring, I hoped to tear up the shaggy carpeting and install hardwood floors, if finances permitted. I wanted to plant another narrow garden around the porch foundation.

I planned to volunteer at the nearby Merck Forest, manning the preserve's admissions booth and taking some nature courses. I might sign up as well for Billy's pottery course in Shushan, perhaps crafting an urn for the garden. I wanted to branch out on the mountain, meet some people, make some friends, start building a life here. I had arranged to be trained as a literacy volunteer. I wanted to keep learning—about nature, me, this place.

It looked as if I might be able to hang on to this place after all; my writing career seemed to be mysteriously on the rebound. Magazine editors were calling me again, rather than ignoring my calls. At the urging of a book editor who startled me by calling *me* up one morning and lamenting my retreat from fiction, I had an idea for a new novel and was writing and polishing a proposal; my agent sounded uncharacteristically hopeful.

I had finished the nonfiction book I was working on, which had begun as a book about Thomas Merton but wound up as this one—a drama of change, a story of running to a mountaintop. I was in the process, I hoped, of selling another nonfiction book.

For me, doubt and crisis would never be completely vanquished, and faith never absolute, yet I felt this turn was more than mere capriciousness. I had stood my ground, believed in myself, and so, in time, had some others. I had chosen to have faith in my work, to accept the idea that it was what I loved to do and was meant to do. I had clung for dear life to my dreams, in the face of common sense and conventional wisdom, and they had not failed me.

To a great degree, Merton had guided me in this; I had come to the mountain feeling he'd inspired me to make the trip, and I returned understanding that his abiding faith had helped me fashion my own. I had dug into some buried wellspring of determination to be the architect of my own life, and here I was preparing to undertake some new books I was excited about, perhaps more grateful than I would have been a year earlier.

I no longer doubted the wisdom of buying this place. I was glad I had listened to the voice within urging me on, telling me it was important.

In the summer, Paula planned to spend her vacation on the mountaintop with me, her longest time there by far, hiking, exploring, spending half the morning on the porch with her beloved daily newspaper and several mugs of coffee. I hoped to spend summer mornings writing my seventh novel.

Emma said she might make it up for a weekend, somewhere between studying in Europe and working in a bookstore in New Jersey. I wouldn't hold my breath.

A few weeks earlier, Paula, Emma, and I had undertaken that dramatic ritual of middle-class family life, the college tour. Driving around New England, watching my beautiful, healthy, gifted, thoughtful, and wide-eyed daughter as she gazed at Gothic courtyards and scoped out the activities on bulletin boards, imagining a future beyond the confines of our house and our town, I thought I might swoon with pride and gratitude.

This was what we had worked toward, this triumphant, healthy, and inevitably bittersweet parting. We could hardly have scripted a more telling journey of separation, growth, and change—or a more satisfying one.

Surprisingly, I was coming to better terms with life in New Jersey. Going away so often had freed me to like it more. I felt more at ease, tolerant, open to people. I was no longer so claustrophobic, nattering on day and night about finding a different place and way to live.

The mountain house quelled some of the restlessness inside, the turbulence created by all those intense and unrequited dreams. I could go there happily and come back happily, truly the best of both worlds.

Somehow, this house functioned as a security blanket, taking the pressure off. Sometimes, I was learning, it was enough to have a retreat, even if you didn't always retreat there. Sometimes you could replicate the feeling of a retreat without having to be there. And sometimes going there made you see that you didn't need it as much as you'd thought.

Each time I returned home, the idea intensified that you could never really leave or come home; you could only haul home around with you like a knapsack no matter where you went. The discovery had freed me.

Soon enough, I loved coming here and I loved going back. My heart lifted each time I turned left onto a country road north of a town called Schaghaticoke, past the fairgrounds, and saw the landscape suddenly open up before me, farms rolling off to the left, hills and valleys unfolding to the right. I loved passing the dairy herds, goats, and sheep, the huge blue silos, the farm dogs giving halfhearted chase to each passing vehicle. I loved seeing the mountains heave into view.

I had the delicious and exotic sensation of having crossed a border, entered another dimension. I would pull over, step out of the car, change shoes, stretch, and take deep breaths, begin the process of settling in. There was a quiet country lane just outside Cambridge where I could stop and let the dogs walk along a rippling stream, before I stopped at the market for provisions.

On the way home, I'd come to savor a different kind of portal, with another kind of scenery. After three hours or so,

I'd enter New Jersey on Route 17 South, the perfect gateway to my state—clogged highway, miles of gas stations, malls, chain stores, car dealerships, and fast-food joints. One leg of each trip brought beauty and peace, which I desperately needed, and the return brought civilization, convenience, sophistication, familiarity, and family, things I needed just as much.

Sometimes you go away so that you can come home or find out what home really means. The mountain had helped with this. Change is clarifying, like getting a new pair of glasses with a better prescription. Fuzzy things become clearer; perspectives sharpen; the focus changes. After a while, what you feel is different from what you felt. You've rearranged yourself.

When I return from upstate, everybody at home will be very happy to see me. I'll get hugs and kisses, questions about the twins and my garden and the sprouting meadow, news from home, work, and school. I'll get to see how loved I am, as well as how much I love my family.

We'll head out to dinner at the local diner—it's Jersey, after all—to trade stories, catch up, reconnect. We'll catch up on movies, go for walks. I'll wade through my E-mail. The going and coming and going have their own satisfactions.

When all is said and done, home is the center of gravity. It's where I'm known and understood, where people saw me arrive, grow older, become a writer, raise a child; where people run into me in the supermarket, yak about schools and taxes, come to book signings, remember what grind of coffee I buy.

I had taken Merton's wise advice very much to heart, as he had paid so dearly for the right to dispense it. Although solitude is everywhere, he wrote, there is a mechanism for finding it:

> There should be at least a room, or some corner where no one will find you and disturb you or notice you. You should be able to untether yourself from the world and set yourself free, loosing all the fine strings and strands of tension that bind you, by sight, by sound, by thought, to the presence of other men.
>
> Once you have found such a place, be content with it, and do not be disturbed if a good reason takes you out of it. Love it, and return to it as soon as you can, and do not be too quick to change it for another.

LIKE HUCK FINN, I have a secret place deep in the woods, and like him, I'm trespassing. I don't belong there.

I should be elsewhere.

I have better things to do.

All the more reason I feel a delicious wickedness. Me, a person who has yet to get his first speeding ticket, sneaking to a secret place.

I discovered it by accident, walking down a riverbank, getting lost. I haven't told anyone where it is. I love it too much not to go back.

So on a warm spring day, looking over my shoulder, with Julius and Stanley trailing behind, I move quickly past the PRIVATE PROPERTY: NO TRESPASSING sign.

I climb over a crumbling stone fence, slop through several yards of marshy bog, then make my way through woods so dense the dogs have to walk single file behind me.

Like Huck, I revel in this freedom. There is no parent to scold me, no teacher to punish me, no boss to get on my case, no parental responsibility to pull me away. At this point, in this place, I am carefree; no one on the planet even knows where I am.

The woods are dark and overgown, and I might be lost if I didn't hear the rushing waters of the Battenkill ahead. After a quarter of a mile, I break through the bushes to its bank. The river widens here, the shallow water pooling over pebbles, dawdling briefly, then growing deeper, swifter, rushing on.

This is the place. I set up my canvas chair. I take off my shoes and put on rubber sandals. I pull off my polo shirt and sit bare-chested, something I'm too self-conscious to do elsewhere, even on a beach.

Here, I become a turtle. There are no predators in sight, only warm sun and cool water. I can sit in my unfolded chair and dangle my feet in the cool water. When I get hot, I'll get up, walk a few feet downstream, duck under the water. First I want to sun myself and read.

The dogs know this is the place and charge into the shallows. Stanley has picked up a stick, Julius has grabbed the other end. When they run like this, racing and splashing in a joyous ballet, growling and woofing, I can't help smiling. I watch like a contented father seeing his kids happily at play, pleased he has somehow helped make this interlude possible.

A breeze is rustling the leaves overhead. Aside from the rippling water, a chorus of birds, and my romping dogs, it's quiet.

A distracted man, I am thinking of nothing but this stream, this place.

An impulsive and restless man, I am at peace.

A man with no faith, I've found some.

Crisis and mystery are just around the corner, rushing toward me.

JON KATZ has published six novels and two nonfiction books, including *Virtuous Reality*. He has written for *Wired, New York, GQ,* and *The New York Times,* and was twice nominated for the National Magazine Award. Katz is a contributing editor to *Rolling Stone* and Slashdot.org and is media critic and technology columnist for Free! (www.freedomforum.org), the Freedom Forum's news and information website. He lives in northern New Jersey with his wife and daughter, and spends a lot of time in Washington County, New York, with his two dogs, Julius and Stanley. He can be e-mailed at jonkatz@bellatlantic.net.